PORSCHE 928

DAVID HEMMINGS

AMBERLEY

First published 2021

Amberley Publishing
The Hill, Stroud,
Gloucestershire, GL5 4EP

www.amberley-books.com

Copyright © David Hemmings, 2021

The right of David Hemmings to be identified as the Author
of this work has been asserted in accordance with the
Copyright, Designs and Patents Act 1988.

All rights reserved. No part of this book may be reprinted
or reproduced or utilised in any form or by any electronic,
mechanical or other means, now known or hereafter invented,
including photocopying and recording, or in any information
storage or retrieval system, without the permission in writing
from the Publishers.

ISBN: 978 1 3981 0668 0 (print)
ISBN: 978 1 3981 0669 7 (ebook)

British Library Cataloguing in Publication Data.
A catalogue record for this book is available from the British Library.

Typeset in 10pt on 13pt Celeste.
Origination by Amberley Publishing.
Printed in the UK.

Contents

Introduction

The 928 has been the favourite car in my garage for almost forty years. It was never a plan, I became an enthusiast by default. My 1981 928 arrived before desktop computers and long before the World Wide Web. Over time I realised that the Porsche point of difference was not just the road holding, or the speed, but the build quality, resulting in the long-life characteristics of all of their cars. Careful preservation is the secret for me and many other long-term owners, and I share some of these owner experiences in this book. Journalists are given space for their opinions too.

Once behind the wheel of a 928 it can be immensely satisfying, none more so than on a long journeys, when the Porsche warms up and just flows along, accompanied by that V8 making its audible burbles. No single manufacturer can claim they make the perfect car, but by the time the S4 and the GTS came along even the journalists of the day agreed that Porsche were pretty close. Drive the 928 for the history it brings, and for its enjoyment in the future.

This book sets out the history of the Porsche 928 from 1977 through to 1995/6. It provides interesting background information, so that readers can consider the history of each model and then feel secure in the knowledge that they know each model's specification. Since ceasing production this car has always been something of a dark horse in the Porsche range, and yet it was created in the early 1970s from a clean sheet of paper and gifted with a brand new glorious V8 engine. At that time the air-cooled rear engine of the Porsche 911 was thought to be under threat from ever-increasing legislation, forcing the engineers to come up with a potentially very different successor, the 928. The Car of The Year award for 1978 was then a welcome boost of attention when the announcement came in December 1977, after only a thousand cars had been made.

The best way to use this book is to absorb the early information contained within the sections 'Understanding the 928' and 'Understanding the Porsche Model Policy' and then move onto the individual models. Work on the principal that the newer the model the higher is the price. The author also includes a brief history of the Porsche family, which forms a unique background to the all-important legacy of their personal development of this unique brand of sports car. There is also a brief update on how Porsche cares for what are now called its 'classic cars'.

Chapter One

A Brief History of Porsche

Any book that offers a detailed analysis about a model from the Porsche range would be incomplete if it did not include something of the Porsche family history. The company's founder was Professor Dr Ferdinand Porsche, who was born in 1875 and educated in Vienna, Austria, where he trained and established himself as a brilliant and innovative engineer. At the age of 24 he had already designed the Lohner-Porsche with 4-wheel drive and an electric motor in each wheel hub. This vehicle was presented to the Paris Exhibition in 1900.

The Porsche factory located at the centre of Zuffenhausen, Stuttgart, Germany. (C. Clark)

He was to spend time working for Austro-Daimler and as Technical Director for Daimler was responsible for the SS and SSK Mercedes Benz sports cars, built for the road. After a period at Steyr Corporation he went on to set up his own design company in 1931 in the name of Dr.Ing. h. c. F. Porsche Gmbh, which was to be the forerunner of today's business of Porsche AG.

One of this company's first design commissions was for a consortium of four companies: Audi, DKW, Horsch and Wanderer. They wanted a racing car that would break the mould and Ferdinand gave it to them with a driver sitting very low, but in front of a rear-mounted engine. The car was badged an Auto-Union and was able to beat the finest Grand Prix cars of the day between 1934 and 1939.

At the same time the German government had encouraged a competition between rival German car manufacturers to develop a practical, but above all else an economical, four-seater – a small saloon car that 'the people' could afford.

This was a perfect gift for Porsche in 1936, whose designs were readily adapted to meet the aims of a People's Car, or when translated, to a Volkswagen. The war years were to freeze these developments from 1939 onwards, with civilian projects taking a back seat until 1946. The air-cooled Volkswagen (VW) Beetle, as it was to become known, had to wait.

Dr Porsche's son Ferry (born in 1909) was now in the chair to continue the rebuilding of the company, his father having been interned in France. It was to be his energy that took the company's experience of building designs for racing cars, and the designs for the Beetle, forward into road cars with their own Porsche name. The first had the moniker '356'. Why 356? That was the next project number, and it stuck.

The engine was a VW 1,113 cc unit adapted from the Beetle and fitted with a crash gearbox. By 1952 the reputation of this little air-cooled 356 had been established and 1,000 cars had been sold to a worldwide market of motoring enthusiasts. Ferdinand Porsche had passed away in 1951 and had not seen his car take the first of many Class wins at Le Mans, but the name of Porsche was now becoming established in the public domain for fast and reliable sporting cars. The reason that Porsche and VW worked so closely together was because they had jointly signed an agreement in 1948 allowing mutual co-operation between the two.

By the end of 1965 over 80,000 of the 356 models had been made and Porsche owners were enjoying 'Driving in its Purest Form'. To replace the 356 the number 901 was chosen, but this number was already trademarked by Peugeot and the company had to settle for 911 at the last minute. This would be launched at the Frankfurt Motor Show in 1963.

As the air-cooled 911 production grew over the next ten years, thoughts were turning to alternative or additional models to supplement the range. VW had developed a transaxle model (later designated 914) that it then cancelled, but Porsche decided to rescue the project and it was agreed to make it at the Audi factory in Neckarsulm, near Heilbronn, north of Stuttgart. It was launched in 1970. The 914 title also meant they could share development costs of that model.

Around 1970/1 Porsche had started designs for another transaxle car that would later become known as the 928. The major advantage of the transaxle layout being an almost perfect 49 per cent front and 51 per cent rear weight distribution, especially on the 928. After the 914 there followed the launch of the 924 in 1975, giving Porsche a sort of budget volume sports car in the range.

Where was the 911 in all this? It was becoming a deep-rooted company thought that air-cooled rear-engined cars could not be made to pass the new drive-by noise regulations and emission controls emanating from the USA. In 1977, only two years later, the 928 was launched to generous acclaim. Production of cars and engines were squeezed into the Stuttgart plant and they ran side by side with the 911. The rest as they say, is history.

The 928 was to carry on for eighteen years until 1995, while in the meantime the engineers were finally let loose on the 911, tasked with taming the rear weight bias and handling the switch over to the 928 example of water cooling a few years later! To find the 928 won the Car of The Year title in 1978 made for a 'happy ever after' ending for all concerned.

Original Porsche History in the UK

The Official Porsche Centres (OPCs) are now a national network of more than forty-five dealerships in the UK. However, at the start of the 1950s there was no direct marketing of Porsches in most markets. In England, in 1950, a Charles Misle, who worked for Connaught Engineering, was introduced to Porsche's then Export Manager (Herr Hirsch) and won the sole agency for the UK. This led to very slow sales and the concession moved on in 1953 to the AFN Company in Isleworth, West London, who had previously been involved with Frazer Nash and before the Second World War had also imported BMWs.

The Porsche Cars Great Britain HQ in Reading, Berkshire, England. (Pat Pearson)

PARKER & PARKER LTD.

Longpool & Stockbeck

KENDAL   Tel. 167

1950

Enthusiasts on Paper

1959

Enthusiasts in Practice

1965

Distributors for Cumberland, Westmorland, North Lancashire.

Still Suffering from the same incurable disease—

PORSCHEMANIA

The Parker & Parker (based in Kendal, England) original 1950s advert sums up the enthusiasm in one word – Porschemania!

AFN was owned and run by the Aldington family. H. J. (Bill) Aldington was the Chairman and his son John later became the Managing Director. They were determined to grow the business. The first service garage outside of London was at Parker & Parker in Kendal in the Lake District. They had been approached to offer maintenance in the 1950s and are still based there today, having long since become an Official Porsche Centre.

When Porsche AG took shares in the AFN business in 1977 it was as Porsche Cars Great Britain, with the objective of a new headquarters being built in Richfield Avenue in Reading in Berkshire. This was some 36 miles away from Isleworth but adjacent to the M4 motorway, with swift access into London. It was only a few years later, around 1985, that the 924 expansion of the Porsche range had meant another move was made to Calcot, also in Reading, and this address is still relevant today at postcode RG12 7SG.

Original Porsche History in the USA

Porsche Cars North America (PCNA) have been based in Atlanta, Georgia since 1984, but they have a much earlier history than that.

The official Porsche dealer in Farmington Hills, Michigan MI48335 in the USA. Note the adjacent VW and Audi dealerships.

Sales of Porsche cars exported to the USA began with an agreement in October 1950 between Ferdinand Porsche and Maximilian Hoffman during the Paris Motor Show of that year. Maxie, as he was known, was an American of Austrian descent so they got on well. He was well known in the American auto trade. He was keen to restart the importing of German cars after the Second World War, and specifically Porsche because he knew it would be new to the market. Hoffman went on to import BMW, Mercedes and Volkswagen, which explains why many Porsche dealers in the USA still sell VW models and still cluster together in many states today. He also had a marketing idea of his own for Porsche ... the Porsche crest.

The Porsche Crest

The author has a true short story attached to the Porsche crest, dating to a visit to the factory in Stuttgart in the 1970s. The Porsche Club would make its annual September visit to the production line, which would also include a tour behind the scenes to areas not usually included for members of the public on the standard tour. I recall we went into the racing department and also entered the restoration departments, and even to the newly opened Weissach test centre. This included a drive on the special Weissach test circuit, as a passenger. Unheard of today.

The Porsche crest, introduced in 1953 after Ferry Porsche was encouraged by his American agent to have his own coat of arms, just like the British.

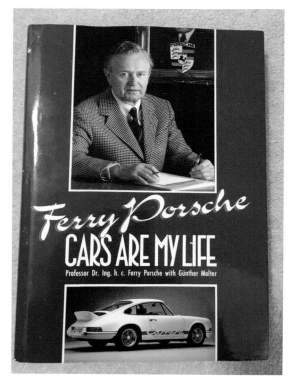

In 1989 Ferry Porsche published his life's work, with an appropriate title: *Cars are My Life*. The author was presented with a signed copy.

It would then be customary to have a dinner in the evening at which, if possible, Dr Ferry Porsche would join us at the table for a meal and a low-key presentation. The group would be around thirty to forty owners and their partners. On one such occasion the author was seated at the same table as Dr Porsche. He could be described as having a quiet and calm personality and was interested to meet us – we were, after all, among his most enthusiastic customers. At the time I had a 1973 911E.

My question to him was along the lines of wanting to know how the Porsche crest had come about. Maybe all the 356 enthusiasts surrounding me just cringed but I was a new Porsche owner and I did not know the answer. Why not ask the top man as he seemed so approachable, so I did just that.

Dr Porsche explained that the USA had always been their target sales market, and you, 'the British', were the second most important export market – he was quite clear about that. When they began selling cars in the States there was a need for a Porsche badge, not just a Porsche name on the car. These discussions led to an approach to the German state government with a design for an approval to use the badge we see today, that incorporates the Prancing Black Horse of the City of Stuttgart and the crest of the House of Wurttembourg. He said that the general style of badge had been taken from the British coats of arms that had been in service for so many hundreds of years to such good effect.

So this young 911 owner had the story straight from the man who had drawn up the design with his Bodywork Manager. I was later informed that the manager was Erwin Komenda, who was the Bodywork Manager back in 1952 when the badge came about. Of course afterwards I was busy recounting my story to anyone who would listen. However, the answer was well known by others who had already done their homework!

When in 1989 Dr Porsche produced his book *Cars are My Life* I was able to ask him to sign my copy at a Club event. By then I also knew that the same black prancing horse had been approved by the City of Stuttgart, around the same time in the 1950s, to be incorporated into the Ferrari badge by Enzo Ferrari. But that's another story.

The Authors Cars

My interest in Porsche started in 1970 when I was driving an MGB sports car and wanted something different at a sensible price. Porsche had just launched the 914/4 that same year with a mid-engine configuration that promised loads of grip, but not a lot of power, as it turned out. They were also having growing success with the more expensive 911 that had replaced the 356 some five years earlier in 1965.

At the time there was no official Porsche dealership in the north-west of England so the 914 was bought from AFN Ltd in Isleworth West London. This is really where I began a long relationship with the Porsche brand. In 1970, unless you were an enthusiast, the early 911 cars were thought to be those 'funny little cars with a rear engine', just like the VW Beetle.

The full title of the 914 was VW-Porsche 914/4 and many parts were shared with the VW parts bin, including the air-cooled VW engine with 1,679 cc and only 80 bhp. At least that kept the price down to less than £2,000 in 1970.

The car was underpowered but it was well balanced and did go round corners on its skinny wheels much better than the MG. I liked the Targa removable top that clipped into

The author arranged for the fortieth anniversary of the 928 (in England) to be held at the famous Brooklands Racing Circuit in Surrey. In May 2017 some 154 cars enjoyed the reunion. Brooklands was the world's first purpose-built racetrack and is now over 100 years old. Although the circuit is no longer complete, what does remain is a very successful Museum of Transport.

The author's 928S4 looking towards the Needles on the Isle of Wight, England.

the rear boot and the sensible fuel consumption. Luck would have it that I moved onto a 911E in 1973 and several more 911s were to follow over the next eight years.

I also joined the Porsche Club of Great Britain in 1970 – club details can be found in Chapter 15. Having driven 911s for several years I was tempted by the introduction of the new 928 in 1977 but demand was so great after the launch that it did not arrive in the UK until 1979. By this time I had cooled on the idea and settled for another 911. However the motorway network in the UK was now much more extensive, and my long-distance business motoring had increased, so the 928 would be a natural choice in the future, but at a premium price.

I took delivery of a 1981 Zinc Metallic silver car with dark blue leather interior, seats with blue/white Berber cloth inserts and the 928 4,474 cc engine with 3-speed automatic gearbox. What a difference a water-cooled 8-cylinder engine makes from the clatter of the air-cooled 6-cylinder in a 911. I love the 911 sound but after 250 miles the 928 is always sweeter on the eardrums.

Putting lots and lots of miles on any car is sure to hit you hard in the wallet. The only remedy, when still wanting to keep the car, was to move the 928 over and use it as a second car. This certainly reduced the depreciation, but it was to be another few years of low garage mileage before the purchase of a 1992S4 in 1995. That car is still in the garage today, in Slate Grey metallic with 4-speed auto box – one of the last S4s to be made to UK specification.

After twenty-five years of ownership it's now all about preservation and a general use for enjoyment at club events and track days. Careful maintenance, plus the original build quality, has made long-term ownership a pleasure, and just as enjoyable to drive. The fact that some of today's ordinary saloons and junior sports cars are faster is just an act of history. I don't control any of that, but in this case I can drive the history. There is nothing better than driving a 928 when fully warmed through and just cruising that V8 along the highway. Long may it continue.

Fresh out of the box V8 engine in 1980. (Porsche AG)

Chapter Two

Understanding the 928

The 928 was launched in 1977 and the last cars were produced in 1995, a model life of eighteen years. During that time there were **seven** distinct versions starting with the simple designation of 928 and ending with the 928GTS. The all-aluminium V8 engine started life with a capacity of 4.5 litres and in the final version had grown to 5.4 litres with a top speed in excess of 160 mph.

This car was produced long before fuel consumption and fuel cost was an everyday issue and only after some five years of production did the first cars come fitted with environmentally friendly catalytic converters, in order to meet the newly introduced Californian exhaust emission regulations.

Therefore when seeking out 928 history it is best to understand which model is most appealing, bearing in mind the performance and the value.

An unrestored 928 prototype in factory red belonging to Pedro Diogo in Portugal.

Understanding Porsche Model Year Policy

All Porsche production history stems from the Model 356 and the Model 911, so it was natural that the format of model updates for the 928 would follow much the same formula. That is to say that each model/version would be expected to last three to four years with an update every two years. Historically the production of model year (MY) began after the factory returned to work after the end of the summer holidays at the end of August. This meant that at some point in September the production line would start the following year's new car production. For example a MY1980 car could have been made in September 1979. Many UK cars would then arrive in October and November 1979 and be sold as MY 1980. Of course many customers would wait until January 1980 for their first registration so as to achieve an MY1980 model registered in 1980, just as they still do today.

The Chassis VIN Numbers

Today the VIN number is a well understood system for the Vehicle Identification Number for a particular model, and the seventeen digit code is used internationally. Porsche have extended the use of this number by including extra codes. However the international system was **not** in use by Porsche on the 928 until MY1980, so early cars began with a different prefix. Look for:

Above left: This VIN number is located on the edge of the engine compartment.

Above right: This Vin plate is found centrally located next to the leading edge of the bonnet/hood release catch.

- 1977/1978 with a very simple 928–**8**.
- 1979 928–**9**

The change over to the new system began in September MY1980.

- WP0 ZZZ 92 **A for 1980** from September, plus serial number.

From September the designation was extended so that 1981 became:

- WP0 ZZZ 92 **B for 1981**
- **C for September 1982**

and so on, alphabetically:

- **D** for MY1983
- **E** for MY1984
- **F** for MY1985
- **G** for MY1986
- **H** for MY1987
- **J** for MY1988
- **K** for MY1989
- **L** for MY1990
- **M** for MY1991
- **N** for MY1992
- **P** for MY1993
- **R** is for MY1994
- **S** is for MY1995

S was the final letter of production.

To avoid confusion there was no use of letter I, letter O, or letter Q. The letter itself is therefore an immediate reference guide to the age of the car.

A complete and detailed VIN number history can be found in Chapter Thirteen.

928 Handling

The car is built around its near 50:50 weight distribution, so high-speed cornering is easily achieved aided by the Weissach rear axle mountings. This allows rear wheel toe-in when lifting off mid-corner. Another major factor is that front and rear is independently sprung suspension and although the steering is power-assisted it is not (today) on the light side, so it works in disguise. On dry roads the grip is very high and provides lots of feedback, taking tight corners in its stride. Oversteer is extremely unlikely, at least at British and most American state road speeds, unless provoked, and the rear axle promotes a tuck-in effect. The addition of a limited slip differential for S4, then GT models, was a useful addition. Driving a 928 on a racetrack can surprise the 911 owner. They might pass you on

The GTS of Adrian Clark with the hammer down, in racing red number 92 at Silverstone, Kent, England.

the straight but your easy balance on corners, coupled with a limited slip differential, can make all the difference.

Using this Model Guide Section

When looking for the details on your choice of 928 model, first select the model type that has caught your eye and digest those particular information pages. However, because Porsche develop each model over time, the change to the original specification is enhanced, so if the reader starts with this first car in the range it provides the basic 928 specification. For example the moving instrument pod stays the same, visually, throughout the life of the car, but the instrument display within it changes over time, including for digital changes in 1989. Read on and follow the development of the 928, as the full story unfolds in these pages.

The official Porsche cutaway drawing of the original 928. (Porsche AG)

Model Numbers

How many models are in the 928 range? Most enthusiasts will probably recall three or four without too much difficulty, but in fact there are at least ten, including the special editions. The following pages explain all these models in much more detail. The details are not exhaustive, but they are intended for easy reading, while still providing the central information for each version.

The list is ...

928/928S/ 928 Weissach Edition/ 928 50th Jubilee Edition/928S2/928S4/928S4 Club Sport/ 928S4SE /928GT/928GTS. All these cars are Official Production editions but for some niche, special models, turn to Chapter 12.

Above: The very first UK development car for right-hand drive came to England in 1977 and was registered in February 1978. Rescued by sole owner John Vaughan. A sleek side view. (911 & PW A. Fraser)

Left: The Porsche name on a 928 was always on this rear panel. (J. Vaughan)

The model 928 designation was hidden away on the edge of the rear window frame. This changed on all later models. (J. Vaughan)

Model One – The 928

The designation of the first model produced, from 1977 to 1982. Production start date was May 1977. It was launched at the 47th Geneva Motor Show in March 1977 using prototypes. The first cars only arrived in the UK in late 1978, after the USA was given preference for export sales. Historically the USA had always been the largest export market followed by the UK. Germany came third as the home market. Right-hand drive models were made in batches, from which Australia and Japan and Hong Kong took smaller numbers. It was a two-door fixed head coupe with rear hatch. The front engine was water-cooled and it had rear wheel drive. There was almost 50:50 weight distribution with transaxle layout, with the gearbox mounted over the rear wheels.

Body details
Smooth shape, faired in headlights, inclusive of recessed front spotlights and front fog lights. Front and rear deformable plastic/polyurethane integral bumpers/fenders were an international first use. Galvanised steel for long life in all sections, plus the major panels of doors, front wings and bonnet/hood in aluminium. Body warranty for perforation for the first six years, later to be extended to ten years.

A noticeably smooth nose, moulded as one piece, with slats for cooling airflows. Much copied today. (J. Vaughan)

An equally smooth tail with integral rear lighting, again a one-piece flexible moulding. (911 & PW A. Fraser)

Interior

Unique adjustable instrument pod that moves with the three-spoke steering wheel for driver comfort and safety. Air conditioning as standard in most markets. Central console, that swoops down to the gear lever and has been much copied. Pascha chequered velour cloth upholstery. Door-mounted air vents were also a new idea. Central locking for most markets. Handbrake mounted adjacent to the door, but drops down out of the way after release.

An interior view. Note the Pascha cloth seat inserts, manual gear lever and three-spoke steering wheel. (911 & PW A. Fraser)

The driver has a comprehensive set of instruments in line of sight, set behind a deeply recessed clear cover to avoid reflections. All mounted on an adjustable binnacle. (911 & PW A. Fraser)

Equipment and Options

Vacuum-operated central locking on 1978/9 changed to electric motors from 1980 onwards. A two-stage automatic Central Warning System with twelve functions monitored from the instrument binnacle. Two types of windscreen cleaning. A large screenwash reservoir backed up by a separate smaller silicone cleaner bottle for direct application to the windscreen. Headlamps adjustable for height, also fitted with headlamp washer jets. Heated rear window with wiper. Powered aerial for radio/cassette. Home market German cars were usually sold with much lower equipment levels, for example without air conditioning. Those cars equipped with air con came with a glove box that was also air-cooled.

Engine

Totally new V8 overhead camshaft (oversquare) 95 mm bore x 78.9 mm stroke with 4,474 cc at introduction with 240 HP in Europe and ROW and 230 HP in USA and Japan. Fitted with K-Jetronic fuel injection and a wet sump. The silicon alloy block did not require steel cylinder liners and runs with an 8.5:1 compression ratio with electronic ignition allowing use of non-premium unleaded fuels if required. Exhaust with twin pipes to primary, a single pipe to intermediate and final box. A kerb weight in the region of some 3192 lb or 1448 kg, depending on final equipment. A dry engine weight of 245 kg, heavier at 260 kg for USA and Japan. Servicing every 12,000 miles, no oil change required at 6,000 miles.

Engine Types and Serial Numbers

All engines are type numbered by Porsche, which is also useful for parts referencing. The first 4,474 cc engine was Type M28.01 for 1978/9 for European models with manual gearbox, Type M28.02 was for the equivalent USA/Japanese markets, with M28.03 for European cars with automatic gearbox. Each engine variation meant a new number, which continued until the final number Type M28.49 and 50 for 1992 to 1995. This M28 reference can be found on the Vehicle Identification sticker in the guarantee and maintenance

This 4,474 cc engine has done fewer than 50,000 miles. Many other cars have seen in excess of 120,000 without issues and one or two closer to, and exceeding, 150,000 miles. (911 & PW by A. Fraser)

handbook. If this is not available the Porsche dealer computer records define it exactly, along with the vehicle's engine serial number.

Gearbox
5-speed manual. First gear dog leg left. Optional 3-speed (Mercedes) auto gearbox, later increased to 4-speed on 928S in MY1983 in USA/Japan and in MY1984 for Europe and ROW. Mounted at the rear and connected by a transaxle system using a connecting tube. Manual Clutch is dry two-plate located on the end of engine.

Power-assisted Steering on all Models
Variable rack and pinion from ZF giving plenty of 'feel', to supplement the servo-assisted brakes.

Suspension
Independent all round with coil springs. The front suspension with its coiled springs and double set of cast aluminium wishbones, telescopic dampers and 28 mm anti-roll bar. The rear had the same coils and dampers with upper transverse and lower diagonal trailing arms, plus 21 mm anti-roll bar, supported by the new Weissach rear axle. This clever compensation meant that the natural wheel toe-out during rapid slowing down, and

more particularly during rapid cornering, was reducing the rear wheel steer, and thereby reducing potential loss of control. It gives a degree of toe-in so the wheels retain a better position when under load.

Performance
240 bhp; top speed 140 mph; 0–60 mph 7.0 seconds in manual gearbox (*Motor* magazine); Factory 0–62 mph 7.2 seconds for the automatic. *Car & Driver* tested the manual at 0–60 mph at 6.4 seconds.

Brakes
Servo-assisted disc brakes with hydraulic dual circuit on all four discs with sliding callipers and diagonal safety division. Diameter: front 282 mm, rear 289 mm.

Dimensions
Length: 14 ft 7 ins (4447 mm). Width: 6 ft (1836 mm). Wheelbase: 8 ft 4 ins (2500 mm). Remained the same for all models. Track front 5 ft 1 ins (1549 mm). Track rear 4 ft 11 ins (1521 mm). The USA had larger additional fenders front and rear and models for Japan had extended wheel arches. Height: 4 ft 3 ins (1282 mm); USA/Japan: 1311 mm.

Ground Clearance
1978/9: 4.92 ins (125 mm). USA: 4.69 ins (119 mm).

The original Teledial wheels. (911 & PW by A. Fraser)

Wheels and Tyres

7J x 15 or 7J by 16. Tyres 226/60VR15 or VR16. Launched with the 'Telephone Dial' style. Note the alloy wheels have an offset dimension 2.56 ins/65 mm specifically to suit the 928 wheel arch. Different on each model. There is a unique Goodrich Space Saver spare wheel, supplied with a plug-in compressor for inflation of the tyre. This tyre is speed limited to 50 mph/65 kph as a robust get you to home/get you to the garage fix. See Chapter 12 for more details on Goodrich Tyres.

Turning Circle

All models until 1988: 37.73 ft or 11.5 m.

Electrics

A 12 volt system. Single 88 amp battery, unusually mounted under rear boot/trunk floor for the benefit of weight distribution. Permanent charge points in the engine compartment in the case of charging the battery. Main fuse board found under passenger footwell (not under the bonnet/hood) with thirty-four numbered fuses, plus Roman numerals from I to XXII for denoting the relays.

Filling Capacities

Fuel tank: 86 litres, including reserve of 8.0 litres. Engine oil: 7.5 litres. Oil type: Multigrade – SAE 10W40; Synthetic – 10W 60. Windscreen/windshield water tank: 8.0 litres. Intensive cleaner tank: 0.6 litres of Porsche Special silicone remover.

Design

Styled by Wolfgang Mobius, under the guidance of Anatole Tony Lapine, whose history included time at General Motors, where he had seen much work on the Chevrolet Corvette and other American styling influences. Winning the European Car of the Year award in January 1978, presented in Monte Carlo, was a welcome and unusual bonus. No subsequent GT has managed to claim the same prize since. The 928 was seen as a smooth and clever shape with a matching, cleanly designed interior. It could be viewed alongside the Triumph TR7 that has long since slipped into obscurity, although the Jaguar XJS does still attract attention.

Author's Review

These early cars had an advanced sporting profile, as originally intended. That profile can now be said to have survived the test of time. Design cues from the 928 shape can arguably still be seen in Porsches being made today. Manual gearbox cars are seen as more desirable. The author purchased his first 928 in 1981 with the 4,474 cc engine and the 3-speed auto box. Coming from a 911 it represented a totally different car, a proper GT. A car that could be taken on long-distance journeys in a calmer and more relaxed cabin, with some penalty at the pumps/gasoline station, compensated by the air conditioning and electric windows and electric seats, which were still the preserve of luxury cars at the time. Early cars are now sparse on the ground and many have gone beyond reasonable restoration costs.

The Factory's own Review

It said that 'The 928 is one of the finest examples of a Grand Tourismo with its superb performance, high specification and exclusive appeal. It has rightly earned its place in the Porsche 'Hall of Fame' and to those individuals whose loyalty remains firmly with the 928, it will remain one of Porsche's all time Classics.'

Production Worldwide

Close to 62,000, all manufactured in the city of Stuttgart, West Germany. Production of this particular 928 model totalled 17,699 units.

Sales in UK

711 sold between 1978 and 1982, of which 145 were manual gearbox and 563 automatic. After the USA, the UK was still the largest export market.

Pricing

In the region of £20,000 in 1977/8, or $28,500 US dollars.

Owner's Story

After twenty-six years of ownership, John Vaughan says of his 1978 928:

My first experience of a 928 came in 1994, when I heard about and then bought this special car, the very first RHD 928 in the UK. It was in a pretty run-down condition and I set about restoring it to its former glory, achieved after much hard work by myself, aided by my two sons. The second experience was to enjoy the shear excitement of driving it on a circuit.

The car's first track day was at Goodwood in Sussex England. After scrutineering I spoke with the Chief Instructor and he advised me to take some instruction, and introduced me to a lady instructor who was a rally driver. I had not driven the circuit since it had been restored, so I joined the instructor in the pit lane, and she informed me she had not been in a 928 before. We drove up to the start light, the green light came on and we were off. I was okay with the top end of the circuit but a bit misty with the bottom end, but who cares, the 928 was driving like a dream. After two laps she told me to pull into the pit lane and said to me 'you don't need me anymore' and got out of the car. Its next trip was going to be visiting Le Mans; at the time it was possible to drive on some closed sections of the circuit.

Photo shoots have become a regular request, because of the car's history. The first photo shoot was in Derby in a professional studio. I was very impressed by the preparation and skill in taking the photos, which was shown in the quality of the finished product. The car has been a star of television with two *Top Gear* shows and *Wheeler Dealer* with Mike Brewer, which I thoroughly enjoyed. It was used for the launch of the Panamera in 2009.

Finally, the greatest pleasure in owning the 928 is experiencing other people's reaction, asking me to rev the engine and seeing the smile on their faces.

Journalist Comments at the Time

Clive Richardson of *Motor Sport* in 1977: 'The power is of a more gentle type, than that experienced in a 911 Turbo. On fast and twisty German secondary roads the 928 really sprang to life, to reveal a standard of chassis behaviour which was both supremely satisfying in terms of driving enjoyment, and superbly sophisticated in terms of reassuring comfort and safety. Understeer is not a word one associates with the 928.' High praise indeed.

The Motor magazine headlined their October 1978 front cover page with 'Porsche 928 - Carthorse or Thoroughbred.' Their road test was a lot more complimentary and said 'Porsche's all new luxury sports car hasn't the mind blowing performance you might expect, but it's no sluggard. Refined engine and low wind noise, but potential refinement let down by excessive (rear) tyre roar. Very high roadholding, and excellent handling in all but the most extreme conditions, with mediocre ride. Excellent brakes. Beautifully made and lavishly equipped. Very spacious for two, but cramped rear seating.'

By the end of 1978 the factory had produced just over 6,200 cars and that running total would increase to almost 11,000 by the end of 1979. Porsche had a success on their hands. See Chapter 16 for more details of the 1978 *Motor* magazine piece.

John Vaughan's car at Althorp House Northhamptonshire, England, home of the Spencer family and the late Diana Princess of Wales.

3

The 928S

Model Two – The 928S

In production from 1980 through to 1983, the 928 and the 928S models overlapped, with the 4,4474 cc engine still being available until 1983, but with a higher compression ratio of 10:1. In the UK the model designation was further extended with an S2 reference until 1986, when the S4 moniker was launched.

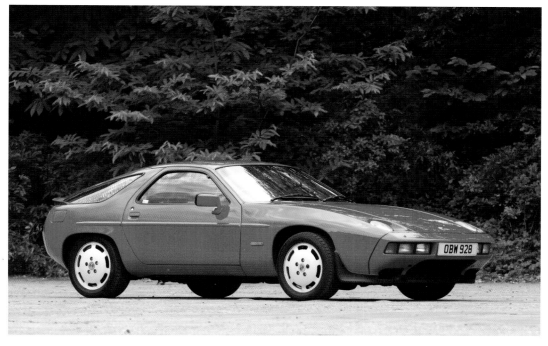

The 1983 928S of Colin Connolly. The side view reveals the additional front and rear black spoilers. (911 & PW by A. Fraser)

928S designation is now more prominent on the tail. Note the position of the left-side rear radio aerial. (Imperial Cars, S. Wright)

Interior with leather seating. Note the auto gearbox T-style lever. This car fitted with an adapted hand throttle, just in view on the right of the steering wheel. (911 & PW by A. Fraser)

Body Details
A smooth shape, faired-in headlights, inclusive of recessed front spot lights and front fog lights. Recognisable difference, now with a deeper front airdam/spoiler, with slots for more air to the brakes and an additional three-section spoiler on edge of the rear windows/tailgate. Model designation is on the tail, usually now a decal in white, grey or black but embossed on later models.

Interior
Still with unique adjustable instrument pod that moves with the steering wheel for driver comfort and safety. Extra headroom is created in the front from redesigned electric seats. Air conditioning as standard on the auto in some markets. Introduction of four-spoke steering wheel (with 928 logo) and side protective strip made permanent. Radio aerial embedded into the front windscreen, around 1984, although this was not to last, and would move to a rakish version on the roof.

Engine
The V8 overhead camshaft 97 mm bore x 78.9 mm stroke became an uprated engine with 4,664 cc and 300 bhp, though only 242 bhp for the USA. K-Jetronic fuel injection was uprated to LH-Jetronic in 1980 with Mahle pistons. This power difference gave rise to the Competition Package especially for the USA. This would improve the performance and get it closer to the European specification. Initially it consisted only of parts taken from the

Rear interior view
of seating. (911PW
A. Fraser)

S model, like the spoilers and the larger wheels, but from 1983 the larger 4,664 cc engine became available to match the acceleration numbers, together with a higher compression ratio from 9.0:01 to 9.3:1 for unleaded fuel.

Gearbox
5-speed manual with improved action. Optional 3-speed auto was upgraded to 4-speed in 1983/4. Torque tube uprated and gearing now higher, less than 2,000 revs for 60 mph.

Performance
300 bhp; top speed 155 mph; 0–60 mph 6.2 seconds (*Motor* magazine);0–100 mph in 14.6 seconds; Factory top speed 156 mph/250 kph.

Brakes
Hydraulic dual circuit on all four discs. New Servo and revised brake lines with new callipers and larger pads and thicker discs. Heavier Anti Roll bar now 1.1 ins in diameter.

Dimensions
Length: 14 ft 7 ins (4447 mm). Width: 6 ft (1836 mm). Wheelbase: 8 ft 4 ins (2500 mm) remained the same for these models. Note that USA had larger additional fenders front and rear, and models for Japan had extended wheel arches. Height: 4 ft 3 ins (1313 mm); USA/Japan: 1311 mm.

Ground Clearance
1978/9: 4.92 ins (125 mm). USA: 4.69 ins (119 mm) – unchanged.

Wheels and Tyres
Fitted with 7J x 15 or new 7J by 16 forged alloys with 65 mm offset. Tyres: 226/60VR15 or VR16 Pirelli P7 tyres. Sports shock absorbers as an extra cost option. Boge shock absorbers replaced by Bilstein shock absorbers.

Turning Circle
All models until 1988: 37.73 ft (11.5 m).

Electrics
A 12 volt system. Single battery, still mounted under rear boot/trunk floor. Fuse board found under passenger footwell, not under the bonnet/hood.

Author's Review
The 928S revision, with increased power, was to answer criticism that the car was too slow in comparison with a 911. This had surfaced from journalists and owners alike after launch, despite the fact there was an order waiting list. The extra power came as a welcome relief to 911 owners who had made the switch to this futuristic-looking car. However, the purists were already saying that the spoilers front and rear, together with the side running strip, were 'spoiling' the clean shape.

Production
All cars and engines were manufactured in Stuttgart, Germany. Production output of this S model and the following 928S2 would total 22,662, proving how very popular it was. The run of 928S for the UK was 2,255 cars, out of which 410 were manual.

Sales in UK
A total of 711 cars with the 4,474 cc engine were sold between 1978 and 1982. The 928S achieved 537 cars from 1980 to 1982. Its popularity had been immediate.

Pricing in 1980
In the region of £25,000. In the USA in 1983 – $38,000.

Owner's Story
Graham Martin has owned his 1982 928S for twenty-three years. He describes 'How I Love My Car'.

What's it like loving a car? It's certainly exciting and it's certainly expensive. Wholly reliable and trusting BMWs and VWs are going to be cast aside. Upgrading the hi-fi system, refurbishing the wheels, spoiling the car with a bigger radiator. Taking the car out to meet your friends, to be admired. Lavishing the car with presents, all to the detriment of home, holidays and the 'sensible' things in life.

Dare anyone work out the cost of keeping this car this fit and capable? Who cares, when it's less than the depreciation of a modern car; whether leased or bought. Buy a 'good one' they say, don't they? But you'll be smitten come what may.

The 928 car design is truly timeless and unequalled. Maybe the Citroen SM is better looking, if not more beautiful. But the SM, well it could break your heart and soul, whereas the 928 will stand by you, will get you through bad weather and long distances, in elegant safety. Just ask Jeremy Clarkson and watch his YouTube video about the 928. You'll fall for the car. Don't be jealous, many others will covet that car. But you have the keys.

Go on, try my car out and slip in behind that wheel, that moves uniquely in concert with the instrument binnacle. Every control is perfectly positioned. Chunky switches that click

Graham Martin's Gulf blue 928S, with an eye for a different visual finish!

into place. Like the Triumph Stag, this car has a V8 used in no other model. Liberated or not, a unique exhaust note that needs no introduction. An assertive sound, with a voice that is neighbour friendly.

What else could you wish for? Mostly hand built, with those smooth aluminium wings and panels. That rear end to excite. Thinking of an E-Type Jag? Oh my, gorgeous but not immediately ready for a 500-mile a-day cross-continent or interstate jaunt, after simply fuelling up, checking levels and grabbing a Sat Nav. Have you actually driven an E-Type? Or just been swayed by the looks?

Reminder again, you made a conscious decision to buy this car. It might not always be an easy relationship, but club members and like-minded enthusiasts will help you through.

It's a hatch back too, a proper family car. Two kids, kit and caboodle, plus a trike for a long weekend at Centre Parcs in the early 2000s. Run one as a daily car, why not? Unburstable mechanics but watch those head gaskets! Gonna cost you plenty. Dog leg manual or auto. Three or four speed? What's your fancy? Temptation came along with the extra power of the S. Find a specialist, ask around. Lots of owners travel far and wide to find this car.

Upgrades? There are plenty, with superchargers, re-maps, racy bits and exhaust options. Paint your wheels if you dare; upset the purists and shrug. My Car is mine, I don't care. Go on, change your 'daily' commuter, or upgrade from your six to my eight pot. It's my passion after all, that's how much I love my car.

The Factory and Management

At the same time the 928 developments were ongoing, a certain Ernst Fuhrmann, who as the Technical Director, had the remit of finding a replacement for the 911. The 911 was the vehicle on which he had to concentrate. Fortunately for the 911 and to aid the relief of some of the tensions within the Porsche family and the management, a new broom arrived in 1980/1. His name was Peter W. Scutz, appointed as Chairman. He quickly established what insiders already knew – that with their help he could see a way through to continue the 911, despite the rear-engine configuration and the likely change in emission regulations. The 928 would also continue developing in the background, as the grand tourer it had always been.

Journalist Comments at the Time

The April 1980 edition of *Motor* said: 'At last the 928 that goes like a Porsche should. A number of small improvements and impressive economy make the £25,000 928S truly desirable. This is the high performance version [Author's note: the 928 and 928S were offered together for at least two years] of Porsche's front engine/transaxle supercar. Larger 4.7 litre V8 engine gives stunning acceleration and flexibility and a top speed in the region of 155 mph with 16 mpg economy. Gear change is quick and positive, but for right hand drive cars it has an awkward gate pattern. A very fast, but still smooth supercar. If other supercar manufacturers are to justify their existence in the face of dwindling energy resources they will need to follow the lead taken by Porsche, who with the 924 Turbo and the 928S show the world it does not have to be synonymous with high thirst.'

Total Production

This had exceeded 25,000 cars by 1983 – deliveries had averaged just over 4,000 cars per year. Sales in UK climbed to 300 per year from 1982, hitting a peak of 383 in 1986.

4

Weissach Edition/Jubilee Edition

Model Three – Special Edition MY1982 928S Weissach Edition

This model was sold only in North America. A limited run of 205 cars was supposedly produced, but one of the features was a numbered plaque on the specially coloured interior dashboard. Higher numbers have been seen on genuine cars. Porsche like to be flexible. All the cars were painted champagne metallic gold (Heilbronze) with gold flat disc wheels and a distinctive two-tone leather interior. The numbered plaque came with a matching three-piece luggage set. 73 manuals and 129 automatics were recorded at the time. The Equipment Code 462 should be checked on the sticker in the handbook to verify the model.

Weissach Special 928S Edition in Gold/Heilbronz. (R. Tyson)

Interior front view to show the colour scheme. (R. Tyson)

Model Four – Special Edition MY1982 928S 50th Jubilee

This car commemorated fifty years of Porsche production. This car was painted Meteor Grey metallic, with a special wine red interior that included striped seat fabric centres with a large F Porsche logo signature on the headrest. The factory made 141 examples available for the LHD markets only, so they were not sold in the UK.

There were 83 with manual gearbox and 58 with the auto box. Of these 107 were supplied to the German market and 10 went to France and 8 to Switzerland, 4 to South Africa, 3 each to Austria and Hong Kong and 2 each to Belgium and Spain, 1 each to Holland and Australia.

They should show the specific Equipment Code 406 on the sticker in the handbook.

The 928S in Meteor Grey metallic finish. (R. Tyson)

The standard twin exhaust/ mufflers, USA fenders and repeater lights.

The burgundy wine-coloured leather interior with cloth inserts. F. Porsche signature just visible on the headrests. (M. Hegasson)

5

The 928S2

Model Five – The 928S2

This car was in production from 1982 to 1985 for the UK market, where it was known as an S2, but maintained the title of 928S in all other. The 4,474 cc model ceased production in 1983. The world fuel shocks meant the 1982S for USA, as well as some European models, came with a fuel economy gauge, but this was fortunately short-lived and removed for 1983 models. Both were left-hand drive only and are now largely forgotten in the USA. There was an S version of both the Weissach Edition, in gold colour, and a 50th Jubilee model that

A Garnet Red 1986 928S2. (911PW by A. Fraser)

Rear name badge now highlighted. (911PW by A. Fraser)

Central section of the dashboard on the S2. Note digital clock ahead of auto gearlever and above it, to the right, a red switch with a white key symbol for the improved central locking operation. (911PW by A. Fraser)

General interior view. The steering wheel is now a four-spoke design. (911PW A. Fraser)

Rear spoiler in three tapered sections across the tail. (911PW A. Fraser)

did not come to the UK (see Chapter 4). In 1984 a single estate version was built for Ferry Porsche on his seventy-fifth birthday, with the nose panel of the as yet unseen 928S4. The 928 estate version can be seen in Chapter 12.

Body details
Deeper body spoilers front and rear, with revised spoiler profiles. Body side strip introduced to all subsequent production. Heated windscreen washer nozzles introduced. The original six-year body warranty was extended to ten years in 1986, at the end of S production, on all galvanised steel panels. In the same year, the USA traffic laws required a high mounted rear brake light in the rear hatch window.

Interior
Minor changes to trim and the seating had been redesigned to increase headroom for taller drivers. A radio aerial was included in windscreen/windshield glass. The Porsche marketing department was keen to emphasise the craftsmanship that went into building the car, emphasising the hand finishing being especially evident on the interior. The engine and manual gearbox were still being hand assembled in Stuttgart.

Engine
The V8 was uprated from 4,664 cc and 300 bhp to 310 bhp and later changed to LH Jetronic fuel injection. The 97 mm bore was an increase from 95 mm, but at the same time maintained 78.9 mm stroke. Catalytic converters were introduced in 1986 to manage the new unleaded fuels, and became standard on the subsequent S4.

Performance
Autocar quoted an S2 top speed of 155 mph/255 kph with a 0–60 mph of 6.7 seconds. The factory quoted 0–62 mph/100 kph of 6.2 seconds with a maximum speed of 158 mph/255 kph.

Brakes

ABS became standard in 1984. An important first for Porsche, the 928 was the model chosen for that introduction.

Gearbox

Introduction of a 4-speed automatic in MY1983. The 5-speed nanual gearbox continued.

Wheels and Tyres

Fitted with 225/50 VR16 front, 225/50 VR16 rear with 7Jx 16 H2 rims and 65 mm offsets front and rear.

UK Sales

The S and S2 model sales averaged around 300 cars per year between 1982 and 1985, from which only fifty per year would be the manual gearbox.

Pricing in 1985

From £35,600 in the UK; from $43,000 in USA.

Flat Dish 16 ins wheels with seven slots. (911PW A. Fraser)

6

The 928S4

Model Six – The 928S4

Produced from 1986 to 1992, this represented a major upgrade with a larger engine capacity and a host of equipment updated. There never was an official S3 model, although some markets like Australia received the 4,957 cc engine almost twelve months in advance, so it was dubbed locally S3. The S4 car finally represented an engine and body that was common to all markets, without having to produce numerous variations on the production line, but came with the inevitable increase in weights and costs.

The 928S4 body has come of age, with a smooth and fresh slippery frontal finish integrated with easy on the eye airducts, leading to new extended side sills taking the side body lines to the rear, which in turn reveals a new set of curves that complete the transformation from old to new. This car owned by Paul Seagrave. (Borg Photos)

The S4 badge
now has increased
prominence.
(Borg Photos)

Kerb Weights

Increased from 3,192 lb or 1448 kg for the basic 928, to 1580 kg or 3505 lb for the S4 (Europe). The car was putting on weight!

Two-door Fixed Head Coupe

At about this time the factory is believed to have commissioned a design study based on a cabriolet version with folding soft-top. The example that was made appears from time to time in the Porsche Museum in Stuttgart. It never made production. See Chapter Twelve.

Body Details

On the S4 it was all change to the front and rear plastic body panels and the road lighting. The front spoiler was smoother and one piece, the rear spoiler became a separate wing mounted onto the rear window frame. Some early ones were even hinged for easy cleaning! The rear lights were now flush-mounted with the plastic panel. Twin exhaust was now standard. The aerial had moved to the roof. Equipment levels increased, such as tinted glass all round. The options list was now very extensive – although prices had increased and previous options were now included, somehow the list did not get shorter.

Interior

The instruments changed from analogue to digital circuits with a new odometer. In 1989, revised gauges with digital readouts for such items as average speed, fuel consumption and outside temperature were added, all at the flick of a lever. Cruise control was standardised and the alarm systems upgraded. From 1990 twin airbags were first introduced for the American market. In 1991 the CD auto changer was included, although cassette tapes were still on the radio specification listing.

Frontal nose panel showing the smoother profile. (Borg Photos)

The full rear body panel is now an integrated design with a curvaceous new spoiler position. It is mounted on the hatch door itself. Early rear spoiler production was also hinged for ease of cleaning access to the rear window glass. (Borg Photos)

The instrument panel is now fully digital with Porsche giving as much prominence to the speedometer as it does to the rev counter. (Borg Photos)

The central dashboard is still standing the design test of time. Note this car has non-standard 968 Club Sport steering wheel. (Borg Photos)

Engine and Performance

A deserved increase in capacity to 4,957 cc (effectively 5.0 litres) ref M28.42 that came with 320 bhp and a top speed of 158 mph (recorded by *Autocar* magazine), with a 0–60 mph of 6.4 seconds. Factory stated a 0–62.5 mph of 6.3 seconds with a max speed 164 mph. LH Jetronic fuel injection. Maximum torque 430 Nm at 3,000 rpm. From 1986 catalytic converters were added for the USA and Japan. Four valves per cylinder, a 32-valve engine with an increased Bore to 100 mm and an unchanged stroke of 78.9 mm. The GTS was given a longer stroke of 85.9 mm.

Gearbox

The introduction of a ZF limited slip differential (M220) in 1987 was available on the manual 5-speed gearbox and the automatic 4-speed. The manual clutch changed to single

The engine bay becomes ever more crowded with the larger 4,997 cc motor and its accessories. (Borg Photos)

plate design. After 1989 only the auto gearbox version was available. However on MY1990 S4 and GT versions was now M221, a special limited slip differential with variable locking, given the new title of PSD.

Brakes
Ventilated disc brakes with 4 piston callipers. Anti-lock braking system ABS from the previous 'S' model now installed as standard,.

Wheels and Tyres
These comprised 225/50 ZR16 front with larger 245/45 VR16 rear. This meant the 7J front rims now had 8J rims at the rear. Offsets of 65 mm/2.56 ins front and 52.3 mm/2.09 ins rear. Porsche's own tyre pressure monitor system RDK existed on each wheel from MY1989.

Dimensions
Now longer by 3 in - extended to 14 ft 10 in. The width was unchanged at 6ft. The weight increased to approximately 1580 kg, depending on the final specification from the options list.

Pricing
On first introduction in the USA in 1985 – $50,000. In the UK in 1988 – £48,900.

The attractive three-quarter view. Cup design alloy wheels and teardrop mirrors were not standard for this car, but are a popular modification. (Borg Photos)

Author's Review

The S4 was arguably the 928 that should have been launched in 1977, as a replacement of the sacred 911. Sometime before the 1986 S4 was introduced, the decision must already have been made (by the then chairman Peter Schutz) that the 911 would retain its top of the range image and position. The 911 Turbo that had become so popular from launch in 1976 had given Porsche a confidence boost for the entire range, but Porsche were still seeking a 911 successor in other ways. This was evidenced by the cheaper 924 that had been co-developed with Volkswagen to widen the range, along with the earlier 914/4 that had failed to hit the mark in 1970. These times were not easy. On a practical note the author has been running an S4 since 1995 and suggests that the model is often overlooked. There are many poor condition S4 cars, perhaps because too many were made at the time and they lost their perceived exclusivity.

Owner's Story

Paul Seagrave reflects on his 1989S4 after five years of ownership.

It's a white elephant; a bit of a Marmite car, loved by some, but not by others. These are the comments I heard before I bought my own white 928. I knew the previous owner of this 928S4 and I knew that he loved it, but not by how much. I arranged to go and look at the car and found the biggest car owner's history file I have ever seen. This made the buying decision easy.

I have previously owned a Porsche 944 Turbo, a 968 Club Sport and a 911 996. So being a bit of a transaxle Porsche fan I viewed the 928 as a larger version, but in fact a 928 is a unique Porsche model.

The first thing I noticed on climbing into the car is how futuristic it all looked in the cabin, a few buttons to play with, heated memory seats in a 1989 car, and they work! The carpets are deep pile and luxurious. Everything is solid, the sunroof opens and closes with smooth precision. You can turn the key and the engine bursts into life with that V8 burble. Then the first drive down the road and you have to squeeze the accelerator hard to make it go, then the car does not seem very happy, the suspension is not compliant, the engine does not appear to want to go. Question. Have I bought a bad car? No, it just needs a good 20 minutes to warm up. Then it comes alive, everything synchronizes, the car is transformed. The comfortable driving position is just right, you kick down the accelerator, it surges forward. You are driving a GT car so well poised. Turning off the main road to go cross-country it's a big car, it's quite wide, it's not going to be happy? Somehow it is, with that Weissach rear axle aiding the steering process. Getting on the power early, powering through the bends, and the car performs well. At thirty years old many classics look good, but cannot deliver in the modern world. The 928 does with plenty to spare.

The car is original except for a 968 Club Sport steering wheel, Cup 1 alloys and teardrop mirrors. I find magazine articles among the history, and old MOTs, and the receipts from the previous owner. He was an engineer. Most people look at the paint or the engine power, not this owner. He renewed the suspension, the geometry bushes, the brakes and the tyres and the steering. All of the things that get overlooked, and it's the reason why this thirty-year-old car drives so well, it's as good as factory fresh underneath.

The car gets great reaction when I am out and about, other drivers are surprised it still goes so fast. At high speed it squats down and hugs the road. The Porsche brakes bring it to rest quickly. Time for a fuel stop and a step back in time, there is no electric fuel flap and you have to use the ignition key to unlock the filler cap. People ask about the fuel consumption, all the old jokes about a 5-litre engine drinking fuel. I have been pleasantly surprised at 17–25 mpg, which for a high performance car is good, especially when my other Porsche is a 718 Cayman S with four cylinders all turbo-charged, which also does 17–25 mpg in the real world of motoring, as did a previous Cayenne S 4.5 litre.

This is a car designed in the 1970s, almost too far ahead of its time and not fully understood, but now recognised as a classic, which makes it still seem relevant today.

Journalist Comments at the Time

In July 1987, Gordon Cruickshank from *Motor Sport* said: 'A striking shape, first seen ten years ago, brought right up to date. Practical, as all Porsches are. Displays muted brio. Breathtakingly fast, but placid and smooth. A glorious piece of engineering for the price of a house. (Price as driven £50,452 including heated seats at £148 per seat).'

Contacted today, Cruickshank still remembers 'this superb car as the flagship of the Porsche range at that time' from his time of driving it in Scotland, now over 30 years ago!

7

The 928S4 CS

Model Seven – 928S4 CS (or Club Sport From 1988 and 1989 Only) (Left-Hand Drive Only)

This was based on the S4 model and was not available in the States. There was a similar SE Sport in right-hand drive produced solely for the UK market. See Chapter 8.

A lightweight version has always appealed to Porsche owners and the factory has always been happy to oblige. Taking a standard car and making it lighter is a marketing man's dream. The S4 was the base model. Approximately nineteen were made with Equipment Code M637. The four works drivers of the time, Derek Bell, Jochen Mass, Hans Joachim Stuck and Bob Wollek, received the pre-production prototypes made in summer 1987. They had, after all, won Le Mans that summer. The total production was originally thought to be 71 cars, split between 29 CS left-hand drive and 42 SE right-hand drive, but subsequent investigations show fewer CS cars were produced.

The 928CS Club Sport is only identified by a CS script on the top of the front wing, driver's side. (Ondrej Kroutil Photography)

The full view of the CS Sport. (Ondrej Kroutil Photography)

The interior of the 'light-weighted' car looks just as inviting. (Ondrej Kroutil Photography)

Body Details

These were the same as S4 but with noticeable CS script on the driver's side front wing only. Weight-saving deletions started with the air conditioning and the electric windows, replacing the battery, alternator and starter motor with lighter copies, and then substituting with sports shock absorbers. Other removals included the sound deadening, central locking, rear wiper and motor, lots of minor trim pieces. A lighter wiring loom was also introduced. It weighed just over 220 lbs, or 100 kilos, less than an S4. The rear wheel arches are not larger than the S4 but to create clearance the inside metal lip is folded flat.

Interior

An all black vinyl interior was standard, but most were specified with leather at extra cost and weight. The UK version SE was specifically in black leather and red piping with red/black pinstripe velour inserts.

Engine

4,957 cc but with modified ECU to improve breathing, which extended the red line to 6,775 rpm. The camshafts and exhaust received further changes and twin tailpipes. Note: twin exhaust pipes are on one side of the rear of the car only.

Gearbox

A manual 5-speed close ratio gearbox G28.55, later used for the GT model that follows. A Limited slip ZF differential M220.

Performance

0–60 mph in 5.4 seconds, with a top speed quoted as 163 mph/260 kph. This is the same as the S4.

Suspension

The rear track was increased by 17 mm (0.66 ins) with spacers. The Boge shock absorbers were fitted onto a suspension that was lowered at the front and stiffened by 10 per cent.

Brakes

The S4 brakes were used – 12 ins front discs, 11.8 ins rear with 4 pot callipers.

Wheels and Tyres

Front, 8J x 16 rims (60 mm offset) 225/45 VR16. Rear, 9J x 16 245/45 VR16. Both with 60 mm offset. The 944 Turbo S had this rear combination first.

Pricing

When introduced in 1988 it was £55,000 – the same price as the then-current S4, though missing some of the S4 equipment.

Author's Review

In the summer of 1999 Derek Bell brought his white CS Sport to a private meeting of Porsche owners. He had a delighted audience, especially with his car being one of the 4 prototypes.

Owner's Story

The following recollection is from Samuel Fournis, the European CS Specialist.

Over around ten years and 50,000 km at the wheel of my former 1989 928S4 Club Sport, I have encountered a lot of situations, most of them interesting. First of all, I was the lucky guy who felt that this model was very rare, and after two years of negotiations, was able to buy this car for an interesting price. This was in 1999, so nearly nobody knew that a 928 S4 Club Sport was produced. This was my first 928, and my first sports car, in fact. Being a MY1989, my car was comfortable and easy to live with because it included the air conditioning, the central door locking and the alarm. It even had electric seats! Also, it was a beauty, in Baltic blue, the only one built in this colour.

The Derek Bell 928S4 Club Sport at Lulworth Castle, Dorset, England in July 1999. (R. Burrell)

Luckily, I had the chance to drive other versions of the 928, mainly manual S4s and GTs, so can compare them with my own CS. In short, a CS is a 1989 GT with less sound-deadening material, and you do slightly feel the 80 kg to 120 kg difference, especially during accelerations. The suspensions are also a little stiffer, but still usable in real conditions. I have crossed Europe in this car with my wife, two young kids, and the matching luggage without any kind of trouble. If my expectations were high, it was even better in reality.

I sadly had to let her go, but have since found a MY1988, one in need of a lot of care. I will soon start to restore her, and hopefully drive her in the not too distant future. As a 1988, she will be more hardcore, and a little lighter, but as I have driven other 1988 and 1989 CS cars I don't expect that the difference will be really perceptible.

After more than twenty years, I still have something to discover. Talk about a hobby!

Journalist Comments at the Time

In 1988 Georg Kacher in *Car* wrote about his test drive in 1988 on the north-west side of Stuttgart, taking the very straight E41 Autobahn from Leonberg to Heilbronn, cruising past the 135 mph mark and reaching an indicated 180 at 6,300 rpm. 'At this pace it feels as solid as a rock,' he said. "The Club Sport turns out to be a well balanced compromise that combines the best of both worlds – a sensibly tuned engine and suspension, with a level of equipment that can satisfy the basic needs of driver and passenger.' He continues his praise, 'the fine handling, with a most communicative steering system, superb brakes and a degree of road holding that cannot be matched by any other front engine, rear wheel drive sports car.'

8

The 928S4 SE

Model Eight – the 928 S4 SE Sport Equipment 1988–1989

Body Details
Right-hand drive only. This model was the same as S4, but loses 50 kilos in weight. The only available body colours were Guards Red, Grand Prix white and black, and metallic silver. Standard equipment included full leather sports seats with electric height adjustment, with red pinstripe cloth inlays and red piping. Also standard was a tinted windscreen/windshield.

Engine
4,957 cc engine with 320 bhp/235 kw with increased top end torque, 32 valves and special high profile camshafts. Modified EZK engine management system. Rev limiter set at 6,775 rpm. Standard spec was 6,600 rpm. Modified exhaust system with twin tailpipes to nearside.

The badge for the 928S4 Sport.

This model had black cloth with red pinstripe cloth inlays. The sports seats can be recognised by the shape of the side of the backrest. It is much deeper and more pronounced. Note the passenger seat has electric seat switches on the side when fitted. The separate round switch is the duplicated electric rear hatch release, the surround for which also serves as a removable cover for the diagnostic hammer connection. (911PW A. Fraser)

Gearbox
Manual-only, close ratio 5-speed with 20 mm shortened gear lever and limited slip differential set at 2.73:1. Standard car at 2.63:1.

Performance
Top speed: 163.5 mph. Factory acceleration figure: 0–62.5 mph now 5.6 seconds, compared to 5.9 seconds with the 928S4.

Brakes
4 pot calliper, same as S4.

Suspension
Sports Boge shock absorbers 10 per cent firmer than S4, with stiffer springs on the front. The rear axle was fitted with 17 mm spacers.

Wheels and Tyres
Forged Light alloy, thermo-optimised and weight reduced. Front: 8J x 16 with VR16 225/50 tyres (standard was 7J x 16). Rear: 9J x 16 with 245/45 VR16 tyres (standard was 8J x 16). Special note: The wheels have an offset – important when replacing damaged alloys). Front and rear offset: 60 mm/2.36 ins.

The 16 ins Design 90 wheels. (911 & PW A. Fraser)

Weight Reduction
See more details in the section about the CS Sport version. Many UK owners were able to pre-order and specify their car and therefore retain some of the comforts that were previously removed from the LHD CS version. Estimated weight reduction: 50 kg.

Author's Review
When this car was introduced to the UK market in March 1988 it was considered to be the ultimate enthusiast's cross-country GT. Porsche Cars Great Britain was able to specify to the factory that they were seeking a near CS copy but to suit UK owner tastes. As a limited edition model it still engenders great interest more than thirty years later. Those cars in very good condition are now commanding good prices. There are thought to be only thirty-three remaining (roadworthy) cars out of the original forty-two built and delivered to the UK.

Owner's Story
After twelve years of ownership Chris Clark tells the story of his 1988 Guards Red S4SE.

I am now twelve years into ownership of my 928SE, and I have grown very fond of the car. It may not be in mint condition, but it is very rewarding to own, maintain and drive, and the rarity of the SE model adds to the interest.

My ownership of a 928SE started in 2007 when, out of the blue, I received a phone call asking if I would be interested in an SE that was 'in need of a respray'. The car was certainly interesting, so a few phone calls were made, checking the all-important VIN and engine numbers. The car was as described, the Guards Red paint faded in some areas, resprayed (somewhat poorly) in others, with a couple of scratches but no dents. The interior also needed a little TLC, particularly the driver's seat, and the engine bay was pretty grubby. But

A 1988 model still looking fresh today. (Peter Kay)

a short test drive indicated that the car was mechanically very good, despite its 100,000-plus miles, and all of the ancillary equipment worked (even the air con!). So a deal was struck, money transferred, and I drove home in my new acquisition. The original intention was to prepare the car for a complete respray the following spring. But the paintwork was not that bad and the car was a joy to drive, so I could not resist using it and finding places where it could stretch its legs, like the Isle of Man and Nürburgring. With that in mind, I am running the car on 17-inch Cup 2 alloys instead of the original 16-ins forged light alloy wheels, as there is a much wider choice of tyres in that size.

The time in winter off the road was also used to tidy up the interior – basically a good clean and a repair to the driver's seat. The sports seats fitted to the SE have large side bolsters, which tend to suffer significant wear as you slide over them with each entry/exit of the car.

Fast forward another couple of years and attention shifted to the engine bay, where I fitted a new cam-belt and a replacement tensioner. Unfortunately, the very expensive camshaft timing gears (and the main crankshaft gear) were badly worn, so these had to be replaced. As there had always been slight oil leaks from the camshaft covers, this seemed an opportune time to remove the covers and send them away for refurbishment, then refit with new gaskets, etc. Of course, there are numerous 'while you are in there' jobs, so tasks often take longer than expected. The down-time was also used to replace a corroded fuel tank cradle and the fuel supply lines. The metal fuel pipes(that run the length of the car) are all available from Porsche, but their numerous pre-shaped bends makes them challenging to fit, everything gets in the way!

What about the future? Well as a general rule, any model of Porsche produced only in limited numbers will hold its value well.

Pricing
Launched in 1988 from £55,970, sold as a 'complete Sport Equipment model'. Options were few, choosing between a radio cassette or CD player.

9

The 928GT

Model Nine – the 928GT from 1989 to 1992 (Europe)

This car can trace its history from the Club Sport and SE models. In the case of the GT the core specification took the S4 as the baseline with the changes as follows.

Body details
Same shape and details as 928S4.

Interior
Sports seats on some models only. Electrical adjustment for height only.

Suspension
Modified sports suspension.

The 928 GT decal was generally flat in profile, but most models after 1989/90 were delivered with raised lettering for their model designations. (911&PW A. Fraser)

The 928GT interior with manual gearstick. Note the change to the clock now in a rectangular shape with an analogue face. Switches to the rear of the gearstick show an electric sunroof is fitted. (911& PW A. Fraser)

A GT from the side looks the same as an S4 model. This car is fitted with the standard Design 90 16 ins wheels. (911PW A.Fraser)

Engine

5.0 litre 32-valve water-cooled 4,957 cc, now with 330 bhp (extra 10 bhp) at 6,200 rpm. LH Jetronic fuel injection. Sport twin tailpipe exhaust system on one side of rear. Maximum torque 430Nm at 4,100 rpm. M28.47 engine unit with M221 differential. This shows in the instrument panel as PSD, which illuminates in green, only when in action.

Gearbox

Available as 5-speed manual-only G28.55 with sport gear lever. Introduced in MY89 with mechanical limited slip differential as standard M220. In MY90 diff changed to M221 variable ratio, designated PSD. This introduction meant that the S4 manual gearbox car was withdrawn. Use of third gear ratio from low speeds is particularly enjoyable with this engine and gearbox combination, when in mid (speed) range driving conditions.

The GT engine develops 330 bhp and can find a true 170 mph on the autobahn. (911 PW A. Fraser)

The spoiler profile evolved. By the time it reached the S4 and the GT, it was identical on both. (911PW A. Fraser)

Performance
Top speed was now increased to 171 mph (factory figure). 0–62.5 mph in 5.8 seconds (factory). *Motor* magazine 0–60 mph in 5.6 seconds with a manual gearbox.

Brakes
Front: 12 ins diameter, ventilated. Rear: 11.8 ins diameter, ventilated discs. Four channel Bosch anti-lock ABS.

Wheels and Tyres
Now forged alloy, with an anti-theft device. Front: 8J x16 with 225/50 ZR 16 ultra-low-profile tyres. Rear: 9J x 16 with 245/45 ZR 16 tyres. Changed to Design 90 in MY1990. Offsets of front alloys 65 mm/2.56 ins and rear 52 mm/ 2.05 ins.

Pricing
In the region of £55,000 in 1989 – similar to the S4.

Owner's Story
Andrew Brierley has owned a 1989 Guards Red GT for more than twenty years. The following are his thoughts.

The GT is a great car to drive. Even in traffic it is fairly easy, with a clutch as light as any modern hatchback, and the flexibility and torque of the V8 means you can jump two or three gears if required. Third gear is a favourite for many GT owners, the car will pull in third from 10 mph and redline at 100 mph. In the early days of GT ownership I made a number of changes to make the car look a little more modern and to sharpen the handling further. Some of the modifications were a change to teardrop mirrors (which I believe suit the shape of the car much more than the flag mirrors), I changed from 16 to 18 inch wheels and had Bilstein shock absorbers fitted. Recently I had the shocks changed back to the slightly softer Boge Sport due to the appalling condition of the roads and as I am also doing fewer track days. Although I am an enthusiastic polisher of my GT and have won many 'owners choice' concours, I also drove many track days in my first years of ownership.

I have driven my 928 GT at Castle Coombe, Silverstone, Oulton Park and Jurby (Isle of Man). Oulton Park is my favourite as it is undulating, a true three-dimensional circuit. With the 50:50 weight distribution, Bilstein shocks and 18-inch wheels the handling on track was phenomenal. I couldn't resist the temptation to push the car hard and often came back to the pits with molten beads of rubber on the tyres! I felt it my 928 duty to show as many 911 drivers as possible a clean pair of heels. This was made much easier in the wet as they struggled with all that weight over the rear wheels! Nowadays the 911 drivers do have the benefit of electronic gizmos to keep them on the road and consequently it is difficult to keep up with them, especially with their improved power to weight ratio.

Andrew Brierley, in his GT, takes a turn at Oulton Park Cheshire in 2017.

I am now thinking of my GT as bit of an old girl, and less inclined to do track days as they can be too punishing. Also as 928s are now entering the new era of classic status originality is everything, and I am considering reversing the changes I made to modernise the car in the early years of ownership. Fortunately I had the good sense to keep all the original parts when I made any changes, so it is easy to put my GT back to original. Originality at point of sale is important. I hope that day is a long time coming.

Journalist Comments at the Time

The headline in *Autocar & Motor* magazine in August 1989 said it all: 'The GT is the enthusiast's 928, faster than ever and with sharper handling, but far from silent or smooth riding.' They continued, 'Make no mistake, this engine is a gem. It has ferocious acceleration on tap but power is spread over such a prodigious range that it is never unmanageable and always easily accessed. Throttle response is instant and it is as happy in traffic as it is blasting down a mountain road or seeking out a stretch of the autobahn for a 140 mph blast. Driven hard and fast the penalty is the fuel consumption around 15 mpg. The best we got was 18.5 mpg. Beneath the GT's seductive curves lies a chassis of immense competence, so that once acclimatised to the low seating position and the high scuttle line the 928GT is as friendly as any hot hatchback. The four-spoke wheel with its soft leather rim offers good grip but the steering weights up considerably with any side loading on the tyres. This car is not for the limp wristed.' The magazine finishes 'This latest interpretation of the 928 theme is a car of towering abilities, its rawness gives it a sporting appeal that has been lost in the clinical functionalism of the softer S4'.

Worldwide Production

The factory production of S4, GT, CS and SE totalled 17,814 cars. This included 225 GT cars sold in the UK between 1989 and 1993.

10

The 928GTS

Model Ten – the 928GTS, 1992 to 1995

Launched at the Frankfurt Motor Show in September 1991 the GTS did not arrive in the USA until after well after January 1992, so most cars were model year 1993. The UK cars were earlier, mostly MY92. This launch was accompanied by the introduction of the 968 at the same show, so this may have contributed to the production line delays for both markets.

A Full rear three-quarter view that shows the increased curvature over the rear wheel arch and the central reflector strip between the rear lights of the GTS. (911PW A. Fraser)

The rear badge 928 GTS now with raised lettering. (911PW A.Fraser)

Body Details
Similar to the S4 but with addition of distinctive of front and rear wheel arch bulges. Porsche had fitted spacers to the rear wheels and an increased body width of 2.2 ins covered them. Full-width rear reflector strip. Note that the first visible VIN had appeared and could be viewed externally through the glass. It was positioned on the inside of the glass, on the upright edge of the windshield/windscreen, on the right side when viewed from the front.

Interior and Equipment
This model arrived loaded with, among many other items, colour-coded rear spoiler, front and rear foglamps. Electric as well as heated teardrop door mirrors and a heated rear screen. A four-spoke new steering wheel boss contained the new safety feature of an airbag within the central wheel boss. In the USA an airbag was also fitted for passengers, by reducing the passenger glove box area. The UK received the airbag in MY93, but only one was fitted. Driver's seat memory and all-electric adjustments. The Thatcham alarm was updated for th UK. Note that a powered sun roof was always an extra cost option! The exclusive programme was now better known, catering for the discerning owner to extend the options list even further on their car before it left the factory. Surprisingly, around MY1993 or MY1994 the RDK tyre pressure warning and the intensive screen wash reservoir was removed.

The interior is still, even today, a very luxurious place to pass away the high-speed miles. (911PW A. Fraser)

Centre console with polished walnut inlay. (911PW A. Fraser)

Now equipped with an airbag steering wheel for extra safety. (911PW A. Fraser)

Engine
Now a 5,399 cc V8 with increased power and maximum torque of 500Nm at 4,250 rpm 350 bhp or 340 bhp. Catalytic converter fitted for all markets. M28.49 and M.28.50 engines retain the 100 mm bore with an increased stroke to 85.9 mm, now on 98 RON fuel. Maximum power is developed at 5,700 rpm.

Gearbox
The 5-speed manual or 4-speed automatic, both with considerably uprated internals. Dynamic kickdown was introduced in 1994 as an improvement on the standard kickdown.

Wheels
Front: 7J x 17 Cup 1 five-spoke with 225/45ZR17 tyres. Rear: 9J x 17 and 255/40ZR tyres and Boge shock absorbers. Offsets were different front to back, with the front at 65 mm/2.56 ins and rear at 55 mm/2.17 ins. Later, Cup 2 wheel design Michelin tyres were recommended for reduced tyre roar. The wheels also had 38 mm spacers fitted.

Brakes
Increased to 12 ins/304 mm front and 11.7 ins/299 mm rear with four pots/pistons per calliper. ABS continued to be standard fitting.

Performance
The factory quoted 0–62 mph as 5.7 seconds and a top speed of 171 mph/275 kph with the manual gearbox.

Author's Review
The ultimate GT model for long-distance motoring, but still cool and calm enough for local shopping trips. Don't expect anything other than a low fuel/gasoline consumption in the teens. Cruising on the autobahn/autoroute/motorway might see the 20 mpg readout but

The Flat Spoke 17-ins Cup wheels became immensely popular. Many owners have retrofitted them. (911PW A. Fraser)

An extra VIN, externally visible, was introduced for the GTS,on the inside edge of the windshield. (A. Brierley)

Headlights with headlight washers. On the top of the headlight can be seen the bulbous glass extension, visible from the driver's seat, to show working headlights at night. Porsche detailing shines through.

this car is not bought for its frugal fuel consumption. The factory marketing spoke about this particular model's evolution as 'polishing the diamond'.

What BHP does this Engine Produce?

That is the question – 340 or 350? The answer is both! The inside story from Porsche themselves arose during the testing of the engine, when the engineers found they could easily achieve over 347 bhp, so to be conservative they declared a safe 340. When the marketing department were presented with the same figures they promptly rated it as 350 bhp!

The Last Hurrah

The GTS became the last in the range. It generates more interest today, especially for the manual version, with fewer than the original forty-five cars in the UK, and 164 sent to the USA and Canada, remaining on the road. The engine and the body have shown they can stand the test of time. The market likes this car for its combination of rarity and power.

Pricing

In 1992, the car cost £65,000 in the Uk and $80,000 in the USA. This led to a final price of £72,000 or $82,000 in 1994/5.

Journalist Comments at the Time

Georg Kacher, a long time contributor to *CAR* magazine wrote: 'This car offers big performance, excellent build quality and a competent chassis ... but it's a niche vehicle.' *Autocar & Motor* magazine in September 1992 gave the GTS a final testing: "Plusher, plumper but quicker, the latest and perhaps the last 928, shows that extra practicality need not dilute the driving appeal. For: tremendous performance, great handling, uncompromising character. Against: not very refined, disappointing finish in places. Compared with the GT the GTS's 350 bhp is developed 500 rpm lower at 5,700 rpm and a

The GTS final factory cutaway drawing, with a unique inside view of all the workings. (Porsche AG)

top speed around Millbrook's speed bowl of 164 mph is 4 mph better than the GT. In our hands only two cars have gone faster at the Bedfordshire proving ground, and both were Ferrari Testarossas, the latest version was the 512TR clocking an astonishing 175 mph. That said it does cost more than the twice the price of the Porsche. The GTS can manage 100 mph in 14.4 seconds but there is no danger of usurping the 911 Turbo, which takes a mere 11.4 seconds. It would be easy to get the wrong idea about the GTS, true it's less noisy than the GT it supplements and totes a more comfortable ride, but it hasn't lost sight of what the 928 is all about and that's driving. There might be more cosseting coupes and faster supercars but none can touch the 928 for a potent combination of driver appeal and practicality, which is where we came in.'

Owner's Story
Bob Fennel, who has owned a 1994 928GTS for more than fifteen years, offers his review.

It all started when I parked a 1994 Iris Blue manual 928GTS on my drive one day in April 2005. The car had spent the briefest of periods on a well-known independent Porsche dealer's forecourt. I had phoned him seeking a 928 purely on spec and coincidentally he had that day taken one into stock. Having heard the details I was over there to view it within a couple of days, liked it and was driving it away shortly afterwards. Having cost around £70,000 when new, as an eleven year old it was mine for a very reasonable £18,000. Once with me I quickly found it wasn't as perfect as the test drive and my wishful thinking might have suggested, the brakes seemed curiously spongy and weak for a Porsche. The clutch pedal operation was curious, a lot of resistance-free travel before biting near the floor. It also gradually developed an annoying electrical problem in its dashboard. But these things could be, and were, fixed, and I have only very rarely regretted buying it. Those occasions, which almost entirely involved the intermittently vanishing and reappearing dashboard display, now recede in the rear view mirror, as quickly as the landscape does when at full throttle.

In my first Porsche, a 1984 911 Carrera 3.2, I had enjoyed several track days with Porsche Club GB so, after getting the feel of the 928 on the road, one of my early forays with it was a day at Castle Combe. Quite a contrast to the 911 in handling and pace, with each having its own strengths, but once I got used to the balance and response of the 928 it was exhilarating and very rewarding, despite not being a track-focused car in the conventional sense. A more recent outing at Oulton Park on a frosty November day was equally fun, once I had learned the track and gained confidence in the conditions, but until that point had been reached I was mortified to discover I wasn't even keeping pace with an automatic 928S4. Appalling! Driven by the author too! But in reality driver skill was probably as much of a factor.

Driving on regular roads is where most of us find ourselves, most of the time. That is where the 928 still displays great capability despite its age. When getting in it, changing from a modern car and driving off, you immediately feel more connected to the road through steering wheel and seat squab. The car seems to envelop you and you become part of it.

On the technical side, in a GTS the torque peaks at 368 lbs/ft (500 Nm) at 4,250 rpm with close to 300 lbs/ft available from less than 1,500 rpm, so effortless driving can be had if required. When more pace is demanded, snick down a gear or two, press the throttle and the revs rapidly rise to deliver the full 350 bhp at 5,700 rpm. Then you're really making progress. Of course those figures are dwarfed nowadays, as manufacturers generate shed loads of turbocharged horses from ever smaller units, but I find the power available and the way it is delivered in a 928 to be entirely enjoyable and more than sufficient for me, let alone the roads on which I drive. Only frequent visits to the pumps, after spirited driving, and a propensity to consume rather more oil than one might expect, are minor negatives.

All 928s are getting on now and, while no doubt they can still be perfectly practical as a daily driver if properly serviced, most, including my own, are reserved for less regular, but always special use, so fuel and oil consumption are less important.

Whether driven regularly or not however, proper and regular servicing still needs to be done and that comes at a cost. But specialist garages exist and spares abound, so I have not as yet had to remortgage the home in order to keep it on the road. How long will I keep it? Well, as long as I continue to enjoy getting in it, turning the key, hearing the rumble of the V8, selecting 1st and driving off into the countryside, it will stay.

At sixty-plus and counting, that's at least a few years away yet.

The End of the Show
The final curtain for the GTS took place at the Frankfurt Show in September 1995 when, along with the 968, it was announced that both cars had ceased production that summer. The (head) lights had gone out! The 911 was still in production despite, or perhaps because of, its longevity. The GTS production line had closed with 2,905 cars made worldwide, including only 646 with the manual gearbox. The USA and Canada received only 164 manual and 243 automatic cars. This was out of the 62,000 cars manufactured overall. The UK received 150 auto and 45 manual gearbox GTS cars. The GTS is assured of its exclusivity based on numbers alone.

11

Models with Racing Numbers/ The Racing 928s

Models with Racing Numbers – the Racing 928s

The 928 had a brief racing history from 1982 to 1995.

One of the very first 928s out on the racetrack was a 1982S tested for an endurance event. This standard 928S was high-speed engine tested for 24 hours in Italy at the Nardo test track. Peter Lovett (a UK OPC owner) was one of the three drivers. The car achieved almost 3,800 miles/6,100 km at the amazing average speed of 157 mph/250 kph.

Brooklands in Surrey, England, 2017. Note the three original racers heading the line-up. The white car, No. 28, is the original AFN 1988S4 SE Sport racer – recently rebuilt. (S. and C. Mummery)

Car Number 1 raced in the European VLM Series. It was restored in time for the 2017 celebration of forty years held at the Porsche Museum in Stuttgart.

The Red GTS Number 92 resting in the garage, with some 500 bhp under the hood (A. Clark)

1983 saw the debut of another 928S, this time at Le Mans in France, that tried and finished but was not classified.

In the UK, also in 1983, it was the turn of AFN Ltd, the largest UK dealer, sponsored by Porsche Cars Great Britain, to support a number of races. They started with a 928S win at Snetterton in the 1983 24-hour Willhire Race. Some of the drivers to mention included Tony Dron and Steve Kevlin, who are still around with Porsche connections today.

Some racing also took place in Germany during the same year, and one car recorded three wins in the VLN series driven by Porsche test drivers Steckkonig and Clausecker. This car was then sent to the States and was driven by our own Richard Attwood, along with Vic Elford in 1984, at the Daytona 24 Hour Classic, finishing 15th. That car is now restored and can be seen in the Porsche Museum in Stuttgart.

After that series it was down to the privateers in the USA to continue to keep the car on the circuits and, with one or two exceptions, the lighter 911 was always going to win out on the day. However, one or two long-term 928 owners have stuck with it. Rarely was there more than one 928 in any race until the early 1990s, which saw the introduction of the GT then the GTS. The extra power gave the extra confidence needed to take the car to the competition.

In the UK, thanks to the support and development from the Eurotech team and Mike Jordan, there were three competitive GTSs on the UK racing scene by the mid-1990s. First out of the Eurotech stable was a mint green GT that had been converted to a GTS spec, closely followed by the Jones brothers with a yellow GTS, and finally a red GTS that was campaigned by Malcolm Sargeant. These cars competed in the Porsche Cup of the time, The British GT Championship and the Aston Martin Owners Club Intermarque Championship (AMOC). Between them they knocked-up their share of podiums and wins. It was weekend amateur racing at its best.

After 1996 the GTS was no longer a current road car, so the regulations no longer favoured its inclusion. By the time the Jones's yellow car was all but written off at Oulton Park in Cheshire, the three cars had begun to fade away. Subsequently, Adrian Clark bought the green and the red cars with a view to taking the best ideas from both, and more recently Graham Saul bought the yellow car. As private entrants, both drivers have found themselves on something like a long and winding road!

Since the racing of the 1990s, with a standard output of 350 HP, this capacity is no longer impressive enough to stand a chance of winning races when pitted against the competition of the 2020s running more modern machinery. Adrian Clark started the ball rolling on improvements in 2011, updating cams and exhausts, larger valves and modified inlet systems. This brought his car back onto the podium and some Class wins in the AMOC Championship. Key to the improvement in fortunes had been the installation of dry sump lubrication, preventing oil starvation on high G corners.

In celebration of forty years of the 928 in 2017, Richard Attwood was once again behind the wheel of a 928 – car number 40 for the Carrera Cup Series of demonstration drives in 2017. When questioned about the 928, he said 'I have strong memories of really enjoying the V8 engine, particularly the balance of the car.'

Behind the wheel of the Red GTS, note the stripped-out cockpit. (A. Clark)

A real powerhouse at the front, the GTS engine is a serious piece of kit! With around 500 bhp aa 0–60 mph of less than 4 seconds is thought to be possible. (A. Clark)

Graham Saul Races the Yellow GTS – Car Number 82

This 928GTS race car was originally a Porsche demonstrator in 1994, and at just six weeks old was sent away to Eurotech for the race car conversion. Race wins followed in 1995 before a bad crash resulted in the car changing hands a couple of times in 1996 and vanishing, presumed scrapped.

In reality the car had been bought by Ric Wood, who rebuilt the front of the car with a replacement spaceframe and got it ready to race again, then parked it up waiting for a buyer while he raced and built other cars.

Move forward almost twenty years and, with the fortieth birthday of the 928 approaching, it was time to recommission this particular 928GTS and maybe get it back on the track.

A race weekend at Anglesey saw some mixed weather conditions. There were three races and the first was certainly eventful for Graham as he drove the car. Following a good old tank slapper and subsequent contact with the barrier in Race 1 Graham came into the pits for the mechanics to cast an eye over the damage, and went back out. The time lost still resulted in a finish, but back in 26th place – next to last.

Races 2 and 3 had changeable weather, with a dry track for Race 2, but cloudy weather, and resulted in a great battle with other drivers and a finish that was second in class. This was repeated in Race 3, collecting another second in class trophy in greasy conditions not really suited to the slick tyres.

'Anglesey is an amazing circuit, especially if you are unlucky with the weather, when you get to learn another season of lessons all in one day,' said Graham.

In a very distinctive yellow, Number 82 seen at speed at Oulton Park with Graham Saul at the wheel. (DW Motorsport Photography)

Behind the wheel of Number 92, note the prominence of the rev counter. (G. Saul)

Number 92 caught just admiring the view. (G. Saul)

12

The Special Models

Special Models

The factory offered the first of the Specials in the early 1980s. They started with the introduction in 1982 of the Weissach Edition with 202 cars, so called after the still-new Weissach development centre not far from Stuttgart. The car had a gold paint exterior

The Porsche Museum houses the cabriolet prototype from 1986, front view.

and came complete with golden/brown leather fitted suitcases, reserved for the USA only. The same year a Jubilee model was announced to celebrate the fiftieth anniversary of Porsche, all 141 cars were produced with metallic grey exterior and burgundy wine-coloured interior for all the remaining LHD markets. More information can be found in Chapter 4.

In 1983, as part of a research project one car was finished with all external panels in lacquered aluminium. This body weighed 302 kg in steel but only 161 kg in aluminium. The weight saving was considered worthwhile but noise transmission was too great, so the idea was dropped.

In 1986 a Cabriolet was produced with a folding roof, but it never reached production. This silver car can usually be seen at the museum in Stuttgart. It was no surprise that Voll in Wurzburg in Germany and Lynx in the UK produced similar cabriolets, with perhaps 20 cars between them starting around 1987/8, with manual and powered hoods. Voll was later taken over by Gemballa, who had already designed conversions on other Porsche models.

The next model we know started development life in 1987 as the CS Sport, of which 19 were completed in 1988, followed by the S4SE with 42, which in turn gave rise to the GT in 1989. The UK received 225 out of 2,082 GTs that were built. Other one-off cabriolets and conversions have also been built in the States.

This showed the continued interest at Porsche for developing new niche models, a tradition that is still evident today.

A newly built right-hand drive 1988S4 that was converted by Voll/Gemballa in Germany to an electric folding roof. The body work was unchanged forward from the windscreen. (F. Sum)

The bodywork on the rear was very neatly redesigned and blended well to make it an eye-catching finish. (F. Sum)

There was also interest shown in a prototype S4 as a special version, called the 928S4 GTE. One car was built in LHD format, with the CS Sport as its powerbase, with the letters standing for Grand Turismo Executive and more heavily sculptured front and rear plastic panels being used. The German company Strosek also produced some interesting designs on the 928 bodywork, by accentuating the soft curves of the original car. A Strosek-bodied racer has been seen in the States as well.

The French market, in collaboration with Sonauto, the importer for France, produced a Kenwood Radio version of a 928 with six cars fitted out with super-high-spec radio installations and a dashboard plaque during 1988, as a result of winning Le Mans that year in a 956.

The Japanese market had special bodywork requirements that called for larger wheels to be shielded by a minimum amount of bodywork when the S4 was built, so 50 were specially made with GTS wheel arches and 'eyebrows' on the front wheels.

A 928S, with an S4 front nose panel, and a body 250 mm longer overall, appeared as a two-door estate that was specially built by the factory in time for Dr Ferry Porsche's seventy-fifth birthday in 1984. This also had an extended wheelbase and a rear hatch-like door. It resides at the museum.

The extra curves of this right-hand drive Strosek design produced a dramatic body that could not fail to catch the attention. Seen here on a 1984 928S. (F. Subbiani)

The Japanese market insisted on wider wheel arches for the larger rims and tyres of this 1990S4 example. As a result, fifty cars imported to Japan were fitted with GTS rear wheel arches and eyebrows on the front wings. They also had the bonus of an interior with dark polished wood surrounds to the centre console and gear lever, plus inserts in the door panels. Japan imported LHD and RHD models of the 928. Seen here at Leeds Castle. Kent, England. (M. Parris)

In 1984 this estate version was presented to Ferry Porsche on his seventy-fifth birthday.

The last of these developments was probably the most amusing, with a serious side. The six-time Le Mans winner Jacky Ickyx ordered an S4 engine for fitting into his offshore racing power boat. Needless to say it required a specially developed dual-water cooling system to keep it all cool!

928 Values

The 928 historical values to date have generally been lived out in the shadow of the 911. Early cars, from launch date through until the arrival of the S4 in 1986, always seem to suffer. These pictures show the two extremes.

It's also true that because of this background many cars have gone beyond what is their reasonable repair cost, and consequently have gone to the breaker's yard. Condition becomes the deciding factor in the 'save it or scrap it' scenario. In order to understand the likely values, here is an estimated grading of the potential prices. It is not possible to accurately attribute a price in dollars or pounds sterling.

- Launch date to 928S 1985 would be graded as Lower Value.
- 1986S4 through to 1992S4 would be graded as Middle Range Value.
- 1992GTS through to 1995 and end of production as High Range Value.

This March 1978 Petrol Blue car with the 4,474 cc engine was the first manual gearbox press car provided by Porsche Cars GB in 1978 and was featured in the road test by *Motor* magazine in October 1978 with registration 928 TTE. This car can be seen on the cover of *Motor* magazine on page 93.

The JCT 600/ Porsche Leeds OPC are one of the five classic car restoration centres in the UK that undertook the 'back to the bare metal' restoration of this 1988S4 Cassis-coloured car in 2016/17. Completed in time for the fortieth anniversary in 2017.

However, to exclude the S4 Sport Equipment and the GT would be to miss the point that niche models almost always come out best, and these two models do just that, so they can be included in the High Range. Porsche actively promote their history, and over 70 per cent of their cars are still on the road. Build quality is a major contributing factor, with the aim to rejuvenate the interest in the older cars by promoting their Classic System.

This offers an ever-increasing range of retooled parts, where demand is sufficient to get that tooling up and running again. The High Value models in top condition can be said to have reached their original new selling prices, with some higher peaks for low mileage

The final restored car looks and feels fresh – like new.

creating exceptional prices. The irony is that the one car that has reached the highest price to date is the prototype that belonged to Derek Bell, the Le Mans winner. It was a 1987 928S4 CS Sport that sold for over €200,000 and had never been raced! It was one of four pre-production prototype models given to each of the factory Le Mans drivers at the time.

It is now possible to go online and research current car prices that will at least establish a benchmark for the 928 in that market, but as always with pre-owned cars it must always be on a buyer beware basis, where instinct can be just as important as condition.

Interior Space 2 + 2/Child Seating
Internal space is well utilised in the 928, provided it is only thought of as a 2+2 by the occupants. The two seats behind the front seats are ideal for children, or adults prepared for a cramped journey. There are no child safety seat mountings but there are lap and diagonal seat belts front and back. Note that the early models only have lap belts in the rear.

Interior Leather/Cloth/Vinyl Upholstery Specifications
The first cars were introduced with Pascha cloth inserts and vinyl or leather seat edges with matching or contrasting colours of the seat piping. The dashboard was either vinyl with a plastic finish or full leather. Weathering has not been kind to many leather dashboards, although that can depend on the climate and indoor/outdoor parking, or exposures to prolonged sunlight. Door panels were often half leather or full vinyl. A specification of part leather often meant the centre console, up to and including the central cassette holder, was

vinyl covered or leather covered. Some GTS models had the premium interior version with ruffled leather seating around MY1990.

The Spare Wheel

Another very neat feature, and ahead of its time, was the provision of a spare wheel. The 928 spare is no ordinary wheel. Found stowed away under the boot/trunk floor it is a collapsible Goodrich spare tyre that expands as it inflates and is approved for safe use up to 50 mph/70 kph. Considering today that almost no new cars, including Porsches, come with a spare wheel, 928 owners are fortunate. The complete kit includes a tyre compressor and a twelve-piece toolkit, jack and wheelbrace. Also included as part of the equipment list for any 928 was a set of plastic gloves and a large plastic bag to contain the full-size wheel that had just been removed.

Wide Rear Track Cars with Spacers

There were no wide-track options on early cars, as far as is known, but it is believed that starting with S2 models the option was offered and often fitted as Option Code 415 with 21 mm spacers and longer wheel bolts to suit. All MY1989GT cars were fitted with 17 mm

The rear boot/trunk space, with its specially fitted toolkit, in a concealed bulkhead. Note the towing eye that fits into pre-positioned threaded holes; one in the centre of the rear licence plate, the other hidden low down in the nose air vents behind a protective plug.

Rear boot carpet lifted to show the Goodrich wheel (speed-limited) and air compressor and plastic bag to cover the punctured wheel after removal. Porsche detailing again.

spacers because the earlier CS cars already had the same 17 mm spacers fitted as standard. These spacers were eliminated for subsequent GTs that came fitted with Design 90 wheels. The GTS came with 38 mm spacers, hence the car required those bulging rear arches.

The RDK Tyre Low Pressure Warning Gauge on post-1989 S4 Models
Cars fitted with this feature have special units built into the inside of the wheel rims. If the unit fails, which is quite common, these wheel sensors are expensive and have to be replaced. The system is often just isolated by disabling the control unit found under the dashboard.

13

VIN Numbers/Engine Numbers/Equipment Codes etc

VIN Numbers

To explain the details, of what is hidden behind the VIN sequence of letters and numbers. The following refers to an example vehicle – a 1991 car with WP0 ZZZ 92 Z MS 800594.

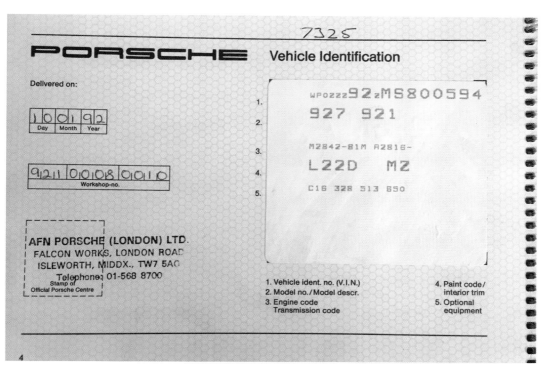

See the sticker in the red handbook, which is individual to each car. The same sticker was also fixed to the rear floor area, adjacent to the spare wheel and toolkit, but is often lost.

- Read along the line to find that **M** is for 1991, for that year of production.
- **WP0** is the World manufacturing code, or written as WP0 (where 0 is a zero).
- **W** is country code for Germany.
- **P** is for Porsche.
- **0** (zero) is for passenger/sports car. The alternative is 1 (one) for SUV type (sports utility vehicle – currently the Cayenne and Macan).
- **ZZZ** is for Europe or ROW/Rest of the World designation. It can be also **JA0** or **JB0** for USA and Canada (where 0 is zero) and **JB2** and **AA2**.
- The **92** is for the car type, first and second digits.
- The following **Z** is a test digit.
- **M** is for 1991 as the quick identifier letter of the age of the car, at a glance.
- **S** is for place of production, Stuttgart.
- **8** is for the third digit of the model type 928.
- **00594** is that car's individual serial number.

The car handbook has a sticker that shows the same reference.

Begin by seeking out the Porsche guarantee and maintenance (spiralbound) handbook with a red cover (silver cover for GTS models), and find the sticker inside. Starting with this VIN number, that should be an exact match with the VIN number stamped into the metal of the car – for example, WP0zzz92ZMS800594.

The two Porsche handbooks, fitting into a soft black leatherbound case.

Location of the second sticker, this time on the rear floor area.

Graham Martin's classic 928S in the Porsche classic display.

The service book information is duplicated on another matching sticker located in the boot of the car, under the carpet on the fuel filler side. This has one extra line of information at the top which shows the production number of the car and the country of import (in the top right corner). Note that the production number does not correlate with the VIN number. Having found the VIN number it is then easy to see Line 5 on the sticker, which has a C reference (in this example, C16).

Each country has a different 'C' code, and more than twenty countries have been allocated codes. For example C00 equates to Germany; C02 is USA; C08 is Japan; C16 is United Kingdom; C23 is Australia and so on.

It is possible to find websites that offer to provide individual VIN number histories, including www.vindecoderz.com. At this point it is useful to know that 928 production types were made initially for only three main markets – USA (including Canada), Japan and Rest of the World (ROW) including Europe. From 1989 was reduced to two markets, USA and ROW. Other smaller markets had their own local modifications undertaken at the HQ of that country's concessionaire, by affixing locally the parts supplied by the factory for each vehicle.

Engine Serial Numbers

The serial number is to be found on the front half of the engine, stamped on the front reinforcing rib in the top half of the crankcase. It is difficult to see. It can usually be found clearly printed on the OPC invoices.

All 928 engine numbers begin with an 8, for eight cylinders.

Here is an example to follow – 81M 50943. Reading from left to right:

- The number 1 is for Auto gearbox (if it was a number 5 it would be Manual gearbox).
- The letter M is for the year, in this case 1991, same as within the VIN code.
- The 50943 is the serial number. Do not confuse the serial number with the M28.042, which is the engine type number printed in the handbook on Line 3 of the sticker.

The Engine Type numbers start at M28.01 and run numerically up to M28.50.

These Porsche handbooks change slightly over time, from model to model, but they each show the engine type number. Adjacent to that is the transmission number A28.16.

Equipment/Option Codes

When it first left the factory each new car came with two handbooks, presented in a black or burgundy leather case. Paperwork can be scarce when a car is forty years old, but hopefully these books have been handed down from one careful owner to the next.

By the time the S4 model arrived on the marketplace the standard equipment was extensive, as Porsche responded to the competition. The optional equipment can be divided into three categories:

- M Codes (M for Möglichkeit = Option)
- Z Codes (Z for Zusatz = Addition)
- Porsche Exclusive (Established around 1986)

M Codes

The M option codes follow the C16 number, in this sticker example see on the line (numbered 5) 328, 513, and 650. These numbers represent type of radio (328), lumbar support right seat (513) and sunroof (650). This particular car also has electric windows (651), but the 651 code will not show here because electric windows were part of the standard specification for that market when the car was built.

Z Codes

These codes appear in the service book and boot stickers as five digit numbers; they were not included on the stickers until mid-1988, prior to which the car may have one or more of these items fitted, but no code displayed. The numbers vary from year to year and are too numerous to list, covering items that can be added to the car in the normal production process (such as seat piping that was a different colour to the seats, or carpets that were a different colour to the seats).

The Porsche Exclusive Department

Introduced in 1986 this department was set up to meet the increasing demand from owners who wanted equipment on their new cars that did not appear on the options list. Owners with models from the S4 onwards could therefore benefit. If the customer requested a feature that could not be accommodated within the normal production process with M and Z codes, it would be passed to Porsche Exclusive. Sometimes a code would be generated, but not always.

Exterior Paint Colours

Initially, Porsche offered eleven colours as standard, plus seven special shades at extra cost.

Standard
- India Red 027
- Talbot Yellow 106
- Continental Orange 107
- Fern Green 273
- Olive Green 274
- Albert Blue 387
- Cockney Brown 408
- Mocca Black 451
- Cashmere Beige 502
- Black 700
- Grand Prix White 908

Special Colours
- Oak Green metallic 265
- Silver Green Metallic 266
- Lint Green Metallic 275
- Minerva Blue Metallic 304
- Petrol Blue Metallic 376
- Brown Copper Metallic 443
- Silver Metallic 936

Care should be taken when checking colours that the paint number is cross-referenced to the body sticker on the car door, which can also be found in the handbook, or failing all that extracted from the original factory records stored on the parts department computer at any official Porsche dealer. It may be necessary to show proof of ownership when requesting this information. In the UK it would be the V5 document and in the USA it would be the certificate of title.

Porsche Classic Policy

This programme is new and is not yet available in every country. Go to www.porscheclassicservice.com to find out about the supply of parts for the classic cars, including the 928.

Now that the 928 is also registered as a classic car in the UK, this 1979 928S was provided by Porsche Cars Great Britain to Richard Attwood for the 2017 season, seen here at Brands Hatch, Kent.

14

Porsche Clubs
Around the World

Porsche Clubs Around the World

The Porsche brand has a loose link to clubs around the world. If any owner decides he wants to join the American club (www.pca.org) they'll find it is probably no coincidence that the tagline of Porsche Club America is 'Join the Club –Join the Fun'.

PCA, as it is known for short, was established in the 1960s and now has 145 regions, which as it says 'is enhancing your Porsche experience, no matter what your interest, be it social, technical or competitive'. They even offer a driving experience if you do not yet own a Porsche. The social side should not be underplayed, for those wishing to meet owners with the same model, such as the 928, in the country where almost half of the 62,000 928 production was delivered.

PCA is totally independent of Porsche themselves, with a quoted 135,000 enthusiastic owners.

In the UK there is Porsche Club Great Britain (www.porscheclubgb.com), established in 1964 with a much smaller group of 21,000 members, but with a quite different approach because it is one club for the whole country, serving all models. Just over 4,000 928s were delivered to the UK.

Both clubs charge low annual membership fees which can usually be easily recouped by the promotional advantages available within. It should be noted that in France and Germany, for example, clubs were formed on the basis of an individual club for each model, which today is seen as being much harder to manage. Nevertheless all these clubs can be taken or left at the owner's choice.

Another good reason for membership, popular with all sports car owners, is the desire to use some of that performance off the road, where traffic and speed restrictions can be left behind. The Porsche can then be driven safely in the Porsche Cup type organised racing series, or on managed non-competitive track day special events where speed is limited by the skill of the driver. These can be rewarding experiences for those who have never been on track and can be highly recommended. They are safe for the driver and safe for the car.

If you prefer to drive your Porsche in solitude then PCA and Porsche Club GB both come with full-colour monthly magazines, *Panorama* and *Porsche Post* respectively, so you can relax in the easy chair at home and just read about the world of Porsche without turning a wheel.

A Record is Set

World-record price for a right-hand drive Porsche 928 in the UK. At Silverstone Auctions in November 2020 a record price of £129,375 was achieved for a 1988 Black 928S4 SE with only two owners and 10,351 miles on the clock. The actual hammer price was £115,000 plus commission and taxes. One of only forty-two cars built specially for the UK market, of which only thirty-three are believed to remain, so rarity value has played its part, plus a growing recognition that the 928 can now be up there with the best of the classics.

Note: The author had assisted in the verification (before the auction) for Vin and Engine number details. The car was subsequently bought by a private collector. (Silverstone Auctions, Alan Kenny)

15

The Future

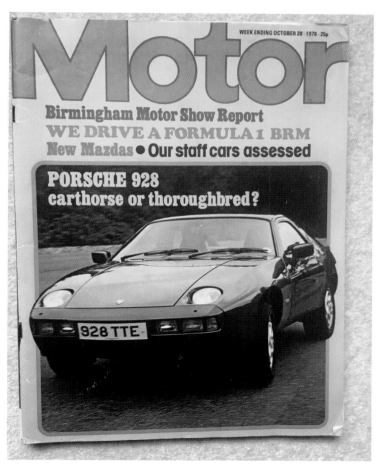

The *Motor* magazine cover of October 1978 neatly brings to a close this history of the Porsche 928.

In October 1978 *Motor* magazine published its first road test of the 928, with the front page screaming 'Porsche 928 – Carthorse or Thoroughbred?'. We can now say for sure that the car has proven to be no less than a stallion, as we close this particular story of the 928 in all its various models. As we said at the beginning the 928 joins a long list of models that live on in the Porsche family of sports cars and now sporting cars, still with the Porsche family involvement.

Nobody could guess in 1977 that more than forty years later these same sports cars would be supported by sports saloons and sports utility vehicles, and that the 911 would be as strong today as it was in the early 1970s. The Panamera is now thought to be under consideration for a two-door version, that might just make a connection with the 928. On the other hand the new all-electric Taycan has just arrived, so maybe the 928 has finally been overtaken?

We shall just have to wait and see what the world of Porsche can produce in the future, and hope that corporate responsibility will still protect the heritage of the brand. Now producing over 260,000 cars a year it would seem that, so far at least, the road is set straight ahead.

Driving off into the sunset. (V.A.G. Sverige/Sweden)

Acknowledgements

My Porsche experience now covers fifty years of ownership, so when writing another 928 book it is always important to remember to thank the many people who have also given up their time to assist me with their cars or stories, or both.

Porsche Club Members

Mark Batchelor (for technical matters)
Andrew Brierley
Robert Burrell
Adrian Clark (for technical matters)
Chris Clark
Colin Connolly
Peter Cook (for Porsche Club GB Archives)
Bob Fennel
Angus Fox
Mike Gibbons
Mark Green
Paul Hedges
Peter Kay
Graham Martin
Stephen and Charlotte Mummery
Mike Parris
Mike Pollack
Graham Saul
Paul Seagrave
Paul Thompson
John Vaughan (first UK 928)
Richard Watling
Bryan Walls (who triggered my interest in writing articles for the *Porsche Post* in the 1970s, which still continues to this day in the same publication.)
Nick Waterfield (for photography)

Russell Wileman
All the above are Porsche Club GB members.

Porsche

To Porsche AG my thanks to the many contacts that validate the background to these vehicles.

Dr.Ing. h. c. F. Porsche AG (Aktiengesellschaft) Zuffenhausen, Stuttgart, Germany
HistorischesArchiv/Technical Department/Photography
928 model data courtesy of Porsche AG
Cars Are My Life by Ferry Porsche, with Gunther Molter (Patrick Stevens Ltd, later Haynes
    Publishing)
The late Klaus Parr, Porsche Archive
Frank Jung, Porsche Archive
Porsche Cars Great Britain Ltd and Vicky Osbourn
Porsche Wilmslow Cheshire for Parts and Servicing Departments – Alistair Nelson and Alan Dyde

Motoring Press, Publications and Individual Organisations

911 & Porsche World (Adam Towler, and special thanks to the photographer Anthony Fraser
    for his archive)
Autocar and *Motor* magazines from Haymarket Press. (Mark Tisshaw and Steve Cropley)
Borg Photographers
Car magazine (Gorg Kacher for historic quotations)
Car and Driver (for historic quotations)
DW Motorsport Photography
Francis Newman, Ferrari Owners Club
Imperials Group Cars (Shaun Wright)
Loe Bank Motors Ltd (for technical matters)
Michael Cotton, motoring journalist
Montage Images photography
Motor Sport magazine (for historic quotations)
Performance Portfolio, Porsche 928, 1977–1994 (Brooklands Books)
Ondrej Kroutil Photography
Road & Track magazine (for historic quotations)
Roger Tyson at 928rs USA
SMMT Society of Motor Manufacturers & Traders (for new car sales history)
The Porsche 928 (Brian Long, Veloce Publishing)
VAG Sverige artwork
Veloce Publishing

The Author and contributors to this book provide all such information in good faith.
Readers are advised to contact qualified specialists at all times. Neither the Author nor
Amberley Publishing shall be under any liability in respect of such information. Porsche
model names and designations have been used for purposes of identification and
illustration only and are the trademarked property of Porsche AG. The Porsche script and
Porsche crest are protected trademarks and are the property of Porsche AG.